PEOPLE
WHO
DESERVE
IT

PEOPLE WHO DESERVE IT

SOCIALLY RESPONSIBLE REASONS TO PUNCH SOMEONE IN THE FACE

CASEY RAND AND **TIM GORDON**

A PERIGEE BOOK

A PERIGEE BOOK
Published by the Penguin Group
Penguin Group (USA) Inc.
375 Hudson Street, New York, New York 10014, USA
Penguin Group (Canada), 90 Eglinton Avenue East, Suite 700, Toronto, Ontario M4P 2Y3, Canada
(a division of Pearson Penguin Canada Inc.)
Penguin Books Ltd., 80 Strand, London WC2R 0RL, England
Penguin Group Ireland, 25 St. Stephen's Green, Dublin 2, Ireland (a division of Penguin Books Ltd.)
Penguin Group (Australia), 250 Camberwell Road, Camberwell, Victoria 3124, Australia
(a division of Pearson Australia Group Pty. Ltd.)
Penguin Books India Pvt. Ltd., 11 Community Centre, Panchsheel Park, New Delhi—110 017, India
Penguin Group (NZ), 67 Apollo Drive, Rosedale, North Shore 0632, New Zealand
(a division of Pearson New Zealand Ltd.)
Penguin Books (South Africa) (Pty.) Ltd., 24 Sturdee Avenue, Rosebank, Johannesburg 2196, South Africa

Penguin Books Ltd., Registered Offices: 80 Strand, London WC2R 0RL, England

While the author has made every effort to provide accurate telephone numbers and Internet addresses at the time of publication, neither the publisher nor the author assumes any responsibility for errors or for changes that occur after publication. Further, the publisher does not have any control over and does not assume any responsibility for author or third-party websites or their content.

Library of Congress Cataloging-in-Publication Data

Rand, Casey.
   People who deserve it : socially responsible reasons to punch someone in the face / Casey Rand and Tim Gordon.— 1st ed.
      p.   cm.
   Includes bibliographical references.
   ISBN 978-0-399-53625-0
   1. Conduct of life—Humor.   I. Gordon, Tim.   II. Title.
   PN6231.C6142R36 2010
   818'.602—dc22   2010025267

PRINTED IN THE UNITED STATES OF AMERICA

10   9   8   7   6   5   4   3   2   1

Most Perigee books are available at special quantity discounts for bulk purchases for sales promotions, premiums, fund-raising, or educational use. Special books, or book excerpts, can also be created to fit specific needs. For details, write: Special Markets, Penguin Group (USA) Inc., 375 Hudson Street, New York, New York 10014.

This book is dedicated to air-conditioning.

CONTENTS

||||||||||||||||||||||||||||||||||||||||||||||||||||

PEOPLE
WHO
DESERVE
IT

INTRODUCTION

|||||||||||||||||||||||||||||||||||||||||||||||||||||||||||||||||||||||||||

To our loyal, first-time, and found-this-in-a-Dumpster readers:
We're not mean people, honestly.

The following pages were not handwritten on parchment with malice or scorn, but with a sincere desire to witness the upward progression of the human race. Darwin may have predicted *The Descent of Man*, but he sure as balls didn't do anything about it. Call us old-fashioned, but our late, great uncles spent decades building a society based on the principles of courtesy, respect, and the five-second rule, and we refuse to sit idly by as a few outliers ruin it for the lot:

> No Umbrella Etiquette Lady
> Incessant Facebook Status Updater
> Guy Who Takes Office Magazines into Bathroom

These offenders flout the laws of common decency, pollute our streets, and encourage the spread of a barbarian social code. It is our responsibility to stop them. In the face. And though we didn't want it to come to this, the fact of the matter is, the whole "United Nations approach" just isn't working, Last time we checked, administering a back rub didn't stop Toilet Seat Pisser from giving the rim a golden shower. No, the shitterati are begging for some unilateral action.

We didn't ask for this burden, it just came to us one night after a whippits trip to Waffle House. Like a burning bush with a side of our pork chops and eggs, Self-Important Bluetooth User appeared to us, an apparition of annoyance. And in the aftermath, similar fallen souls started popping up everywhere. So we decided to take matters into our own hands. Literally. Get it? Because of the face punching? Never mind.

In this book you will find the most wretched demonstrations of moral conduct visible to the naked eye. Some invisible ones too (see the article on Ghosts). Yes, you've boarded the jerk train. Next stop Shinerville.

Choo chooooo!

RESPONSIBILITY CONTRACT

Hello.

Welcome to *People Who Deserve It*, the book. This is a safe place. Here, you can feel comfortable admitting your deep-seated resentment for a hefty portion of the population. But you can't actually punch people in the face. Because it's rude and illegal and would contradict our brooding, tormented inner rage.

So, before continuing on, please sign the attached agreement absolving us from any unruly activities and/or legal responsibility for your inability to take a joke.

I, _____ , have a high enough IQ to realize any reference to face punching contained henceforth is metaphorical and should not be taken literally. In the advent of my sudden vapidness, I absolve the authors of *People Who Deserve It* of any responsibility regarding my behavior during or post book consumption.

Signature _____ Date _____

DIRECTORY OF PUNCHES

||||||||||||||||||||||||||||||||||||||||||||||||||||||||||||||||||||||||||||||||||||||||||||||||||||||||||||

As you prepare to do your civic duty, it helps to know what weapons are in your arsenal. Not every scourge of the earth likes to dine on the same knuckle sandwich.

Right Hook

A classic go-to, the Right Hook was originally made famous by Eze-kiel Shabnef in 345 BC, who used it to settle an argument about fig prices and frankincense stock. Ever since, the R. Bag has served the human race well, leaving imprints from Macedonia to Michigan.

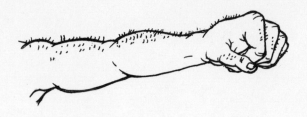

Southpaw

A lefty's Right Hook, the Southpaw incorporates much of the same technique as its brethren from the right, it just happens to be a little more liberal with its application, ensuring Medicare covers your jaw replacement. Penned by the original Will Hunting, before Matt Damon was even a twitch in his mother's uterus.

Uppercut

Looking to take a sucker by surprise, Moishe Cohen crafted this Hail Mary after an Ottoman stole his last unicorn goat. The Uppercut pairs best with a vintage "Hey, look over here!" or "Your shoe's untied!" Then BAM! A perfect 55-degree approach with a rich body and smooth finish leaves everyone feeling warm and fuzzy.

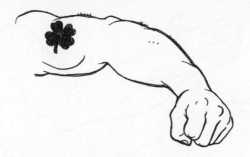

Old Irish

Should you ever find yourself in 1928 Dublin or a Dropkick Murphys jamboree, you probably want to familiarize yourself with this lucky charm. Characterized by its fist-forward approach, ye Old Irish is perfect for knocking out the leprechaun who keeps trying to get his dirty paws on the pot of gold in your pants. You can thank Saint Patty for this one.

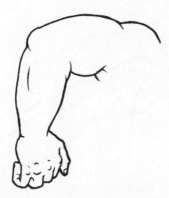

Hammer

Brought to us by the Nordic God Thor in the year AD 1982, the Hammer is an uppercut in bizzaro land. While dropping the hammer is a relatively easy task, remember this tool really only works when you have the height advantage, so either drop it on a shorter person, or face the wrath of Manute Bol.

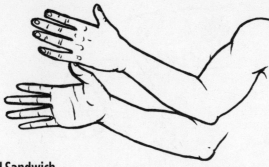

Open-Faced Sandwich

Like its name implies, the Open-Faced Sandwich hides nothing. Two hands, one face, lettuce, mayo, and bruised cheeks. A favorite of foodies, females, and the French, the OFS leaves a mug stinging worse than a Tabasco–horseradish–Genoa salami hoagie with extra wasabi, only with half the calories.

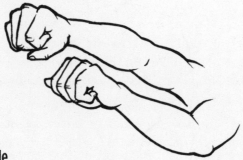

Double Trouble

If Doublemint gum, *The Parent Trap*, and porn have taught us anything, it's that two is always better than one. Same applies to putting a Slow Walker Sidewalk Blocker in their place. Double Trouble takes the amazing punching power of one jab and combines it with another for no extra cost. Like ordering anything from Double Pizza (the pizza place that gives you doubles!).

Hurricane

Coined by the great Anders Celsius after a scuffle at the Annual Meteorologist Awards of 1722, the Hurricane packs some serious punching. Much like its weather namesake, the technique has a range of categories. A lunch at the Red Lobster may be cause for a category three (three rotations); a night in Jersey, category four; and a weekend in Daytona? You guessed it, five rotations, complete with a bruise so intense, it'll make up for the tanning the spring breaker missed.

PEOPLE, PLACES, AND THINGS WHO DESERVE IT

Hooray! You've managed to make it all the way to the actual start of the book without being bored enough to trash it in favor of finally finishing that macaroni scale model of the 1976 GOP convention you've been working on since sixth grade.

And boy, are you in for a treat, because in this section lies the culmination of years of mediocre work, including:

- People Who Deserve It: The O.G.—Socially responsible reasons to punch someone in the face.
- People Who Don't Deserve It: For every one million assholes exists a baby Jesus who deserves a Fruit Roll-Up.
- History of People Who Deserve It: A chronological account of famous hosers since the Big Bang.
- International People Who Deserve It: Degeneracy doesn't discriminate.
- People Who Deserve It Through Time: Eventually, someone will invent a time machine. So get ready, because the past and the future are equally littered with heinousness.
- Polls and Graphs: Pictures! Serious ones!

Olé.

SELF-IMPORTANT BLUETOOTH GUY

Hey there, buddy, we see you got one of those fancy cyborg ear attachments for your cellular telephone. You must be pretty important.

Wait a second, are you even on the phone right now? Liar! You're just traipsing around with a blinking light in your ear like a metrosexual robot after an all-night rave at Circuit City. If Rick Hansen can make it around the world with no legs, you can answer your Sony Ericsson Walkman while waving your glow-in-the-dark coupons like the rest of us.

Honestly, unless you're a police dispatcher, the inventor of Indian call centers, or a South Beach tribal tattoo removal specialist, there's no way you're getting enough calls to justify sporting that glorified techno-earring. So do us all a favor: Take the douche-aid out of your ear and rejoin regular society. Otherwise, it's open season and our fist-to-face connection is one call that always goes through. Can you hear us now?

Right now, 62 percent of the world's population does not have access to hot water. Lucky schmucks. Sure, bathing in the Ganges may not be ideal, what with the floaters and rotting sea monsters, but at least millions of rural Indians are spared the introduction to Hot Water User-Upper, the roomie/neighbor/cell mate/Nana who stands under the showerhead longer than Pauly Shore at an unattended Slurpee machine.

Curious individuals might wonder what this steam hog is doing for so long in the skin washer. And rightly so, because unless the person is hot-boxing a 32-ounce blunt, there is no excuse for the amount of scalding bathwater being wasted. And how are the rest of us supposed to practice our Bonnie Raitt karaoke number if we're busy shielding our nipples from the Arctic Sea?

Should you follow Hot Water User-Upper on the morning roster, go loco on his raisin ass with a double toilet flushing to the frontal loofah. And if you have some of that fancy, post-1800s plumbing, you can always wait till you hear the soap drop and give the waster a different kind of cleanse.

D ear Grocery Store Check Writer,
   Did you know that debit cards are just checks made out of plastic? Cool, huh? God made them when he realized how annoying it was to stand behind someone while she searched for a pen in her giant pleather purse, only to then take three cracks at spelling CVS properly.

What's the deal, lady? You're not even 102 years old. If we wanted to wait in line for our allotted canned corn, we would have hit up the Whole Foods in Havana. And unless you're planning on bailing out everybody in aisle six, your ego's writing checks your body can't cash.

You may think your old-fashioned act is cute, but if you don't get with the times soon, you're going to get acquainted with plastic the hard way—from the surgeon who puts your face back together.

Used to be that flying was limited to only the most elite members of society. Passengers sporting spiffy hats and dripping with pearls would mingle among the sky aisles, chuffing menthols and nibbling on the airline's adorable dehydrated offerings, all in the hopes of meeting a blue blood and joining the ranks of the mysterious new mile-high club.

No more. Yesterday's Ingrid Bergman has been replaced by the monochromatic Juicy sweat-suit-clad housewife who squishes in next to you, only to whip out a Manchu Wok takeout bag full of what can only be the feces of human feces. The smell proceeds to fill the air capsule like the smoke monster on *Lost* after a lunch at the halal cart for the homeless. You could try to reach for the oxygen mask, but everyone knows those are just there for show.

What to do with Fast-Food Flyer? Do we let her off the hook for thinking ahead and avoiding the compartmentalized chicken Florentine and corn brownie provided by the fugly stewardess? Or do we bust a cap in her egg roll for tainting the next six hours of our lives with the faint odor of Genghis Khan's Mongolian barbecued jockstrap? Yup, she's mu-shu.

GUY WHO TAKES OFFICE MAGAZINES INTO BATHROOMS

nitially brought to our attention by a guy named Mike from Buffalo, Guy Who Takes Office Magazines into Bathrooms has been popping up on our radar like Somali pirates off the coast of Africa. There are many reasons this deuce deserves it, but we'll focus on three:

1. It's grossatating. If we wanted to share in your bathroom experience, we'd do what we normally do and offer to wipe.

2. It's really effing grossatating. Seriously, the only thing that should come back from the porcelain palace is you. The magazine we read at lunch should never be exposed to your airborne particles of poo.

3. Crinklage. Not only is this a telltale sign that the magazine has been to the bathroom, it adds unnecessary wrinkles to Liza Minelli's face. And that's confusing.

If you happen to have your own Guy Who Takes Office Magazines into Bathrooms, remind him that the next time he thinks about dragging *Cruising Quarterly* into the office outhouse, we're gonna subscribe to 12 issues of *Bleeding Knuckle Face Monthly*.

PEOPLE WHO
DON'T
DESERVE IT

For every one million assholes exists a
baby Jesus who deserves a Fruit Roll-Up.

PERSON WHO TURNS IN CELL PHONE

Know what sucks? Losing your cell phone. Know what sucks balls? Losing your cell phone and having some jackass ring up every psychic line in Bangladesh on your bejeweled Kyocera. Hence, our undying affection for the saint who returns our baby free of harm. Who doesn't go through our address book. Who leaves our sexting archive alone and decides not to sell our Sidekick to an Al Qaeda sleeper cell.

That's right, Person Who Turns in Cell Phone. We love you. And depending on which way you swing, we may love you a long time. Next time we find one of you magical gnomes returning the mobile we lost after a 72-hour bender with Willem Dafoe, you'd better believe you are getting some serious :*. TTYL.

PUNCHABILITY BY CITY

① SHANGHAI ② NEW YORK ③ LONDON ④ CHARLOTTETOWN, P.E.I. ⑤ TOKYO

INACCURATE WIKIPEDIA CONTRIBUTOR

As we speak, a little girl in Guatemala is writing a report on the mating rituals of iguanas. At this same moment, an unemployed 42-year-old porn director from Ohio is sitting in front of his Acer in a mustard-stained wifebeater, tripping out on WD-40 as he edits the Wikipedia entry about iguanas. And unless the little reptiles really are Clint Eastwood's descendants, that Guatemalan kid is going to fail.

What happened to trust, people? In this digital age, where pederasts and tweeters clog our intertubes, is it too much to ask for some decency when it comes to the iguana sex? Inaccurate Wikipedia Contributor thinks so. Instead, he takes advantage of the system, corrupting the minds of his fellow man, like Tony Robbins at a can-opener conference for knife salesmen.

Should you locate this purveyor of misinformation, fill his head with something more substantial, like the Encyclopedia Fistannica, fourth edition.

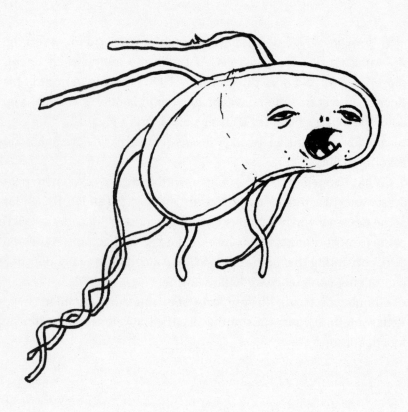

E. COLI

With the all the war, poverty, and Tickle Me Elmo Xtremes out there, it's nice to know some things are still good in this world. Take for example a perfectly cooked beef burger with a side of fries and tossed house salad—yummers. What could possibly go wrong with . . . Wait . . . E. coli who? Poison, paralysis, and death between two all-white sesame seed buns! Mother. Fucker. Is nothing sacred on this partially green earth? Next, you'll tell us the Chuck E. Cheese ball room is primed for perverts.

Yo, E., if you are going to mess with someone's insides worse than a Coney Island Tilt-A-Whirl, at least be man enough to stand up and face the poor sap. Don't hide in what looks like sufficiently washed lettuce, patiently playing Sudoku, waiting for the next helpless sucker to crave a chicken Caesar twister. That's just cowardly. Didn't Mama and Papa Coli teach you anything? You sound like the kind of disease that steals the last beer at the party and blames it on meningitis.

Luckily for you, EC, we haven't quite figured out how to knuckle wrap the face of a microscopic organism. But don't go getting all cocky, because as soon as we hack the NASA mainframe, decode the advanced mathematics, build that device from *Honey, I Shrunk the Kids*, shrink ourselves, and find out where you live, it's going to be man vs. membrane. And fist always beats simple cell wall.

OVERLY SELF-RIGHTEOUS VEGAN

isten up, vegans. We have nothing against your people. We want to like you, and we respect your commitment to making rubbery substances taste vaguely of meat. But some of your cronies are making us feel bad for enjoying the succulent flavor of grain-fed, humanely raised animal flesh.

It's okay if you think meat is murder, or if you never saw *The Lion King* and therefore have no understanding of the circle of life. Just don't interrupt our peaceful lunch with your unsolicited moral lunacy. We don't barge in on your seitan dinners, reciting stories from the slaughterhouse, and we expect the same kind of consideration in return.

If you happen to be Overly Self-Righteous Vegan, consider yourself warned. Because the next time you open your organic trapdoor, there's gonna be blood, and PETA won't be there to hear you scream.

Nobody likes a faker. Think about it: When you found out the mall Santa was just a drunken janitor with a taste for Mango Malibu, you were pissed off, right? Or when Rachael Johnson's sixth-grade lady lumps turned out to be Kleenex cones, blimey, you were m-a-d, yes? Well, guess what? Just because you sprout some short and curlies doesn't mean the frauds get waxed.

Don't believe us? Ask anyone who's played Hide the Sausage with Fake Orgasmer. Or better yet, ask her friends who congregate the next morning over fat-free blueberry muffins to discuss the dimness of your light saber. Just when you think you've brought your A game, Twitter suddenly broadcasts that FO's performance was about as genuine as Captain Hook's attempt not to bone a hooker.

What the Screen Actors Guild? We have enough trouble finding offline connections as it is. The last thing we need is to discover your Mount Saint Helens's impression felt more like the Canadian prairies in your mind. Spare us the act, because the truth may hurt, but not as much as a right hook to your facial performance pieces.

PEOPLE
WHO DESERVE IT
THROUGH TIME

Eventually, someone will invent a time machine. So get ready, because the past and the future are equally littered with heinousness.

B oy, men have done some pretty shitty things throughout history. Call it cooch envy, or too much Monster Energy drink. Whatever the reason, at least 97 percent of people who deserve it definitely have something swinging between their legs. Case in penis—Witch Hunter, the Middle Ages nut ball who earned his pork skins cutting down women who used their brains for something more than getting knocked up.

Boo, Witch Hunter! Just because the Church tells you to snuff out all *chiquitas* with smarts, doesn't mean you should. If the Lord's house told you to have sex with little boys, you wouldn't . . . Oh, wait. Forget it. Point is, you suck hard, and if we ever do get that time machine in our basement to stop sending us to 1973, we're going to cast a couple spells right down your trachea.

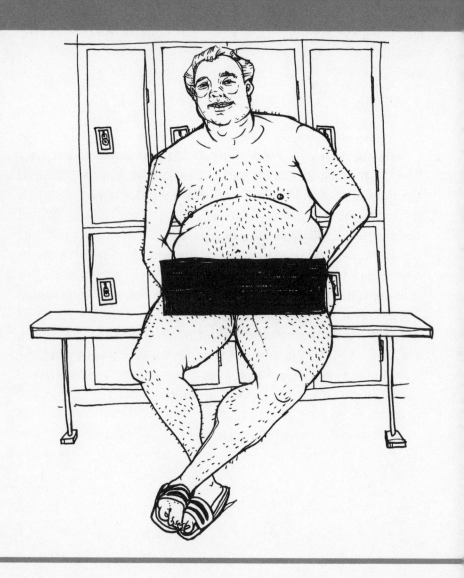

EXCESSIVELY NUDE LOCKER-ROOM DOMINATOR

Let's get one thing straight. We're not against basic nudity in the locker room. It's not like we haven't seen it before. (Two words for ya: Bangkok Ping-Pong.) But what really chaps our thighs is the guy who treats the gym like his own personal super-nude Roman bathhouse with an extra side of naked.

There you are, trying to mind your own business, when out of nowhere Excessively Nude Locker-Room Dominator seizes control of the area with a display of buck that puts even porn legend Rocco Siffredi to shame. Even if you manage to avert your eyes for the strutting, stretching, and Sudoku, the minute you let your guard down, this walking skin sack saddles up with a trunk full of Gold Bond and a hankering to talk foreign affairs. How diplomatic.

If your own health club happens to be haunted by a birthday suit abuser, do everyone a favor and show this corn hole that it's better to cover up with a couple of towels than a hundred bruises.

Walking is awesome. It reminds us of our superior genetic code, allows us to distinguish ourselves with unique hip pops and ass sways, and is a great source of exercise after a long day of perpetual Gawker refreshing and Olestra-sponsored Hulu clips. But some walkers ruin it for everyone.

Presenting Heel Kicker, the Sasquatch riding your back like an uncoordinated parasite who feeds on the dead skin cells scraped off with every giant stride. It doesn't matter if you are Gandhi and late for a puppy cuddle; bang on our calves one more time with your steel-toed Sorels, and we're going to pee in your eye and leave you blind in a pool of our ankle sauce.

Take heed, ankle assassin. Knock our feet out from under us again and we'll give you the opportunity to do what is right—shove your own size 16 clodhopper up your colon. Don't worry, Obamacare will cover it.

CRIES AT ANYTHING GIRL

Every morning, millions of us sit down at our computing devices to read the news. Turns out, there's a lot of shit to cry about—Chinese gymnasts, Roger Ebert's face, pistachio nuts—but for the sake of humanity, we suck back the tears and toast a bagel.

But some people just can't hold it together. Like Cries at Anything Girl, the sour pussy who's had onion eyes for the last 22 years and breaks down when the Wheat Thins run out. In the words of Xzibit: Bitch, please. If a Somali pirate can grin his way to the electric chair, you can put on the brakes when you lose your lip gloss. Honestly, John Lennon could rise from the grave, reunite the Beatles, cure HIV, and win a World Series for the Cubbies, and CAG would still find a reason to turn on the waterworks.

Next time this saddlebag finds a gray hair and the clouds start forming in Crazytown, give her something real to cry about. And we're not talking about the last scene in *Seabiscuit*.

SPECIAL ENTRY!

PEOPLE WHO
DON'T
DESERVE IT

For every one million assholes exists a
baby Jesus who deserves a Fruit Roll-Up.

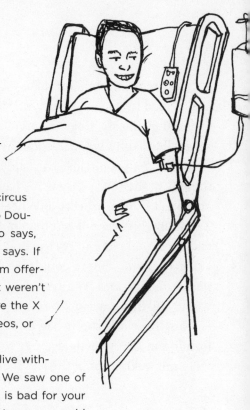

DOUBLE KIDNEY DONOR

Some people go above and beyond the call of duty—astronauts
who give aliens mouth-to-mouth,
one-armed strip club janitors, and circus
bears. But all pale in comparison to Double Kidney Donor, the cherub who says,
"Fuck it, I don't care what science says. If
someone needs both my k-bags, I'm offering them up." You go, big guy. If it weren't
for people like you, we'd never have the X
Games, 89 percent of YouTube videos, or
teaching cadavers.

Sure, doctors will say you can't live without kidneys, but those fuckers lie. We saw one of
them on TV claiming that smoking is bad for your
lungs! So, keep cracking open that sternum, our old
faithful friend, because to you we have already do-
nated our heart.

POLL #2

PUNCHEE DEMOGRAPHICS

GENDER:
59%
38%
3%
AGE:
0-17 12%
18-34 32%
35-54 30%
55-70 19%
RIP
7%
AFFINITY FOR TUNA SALAD:
28%
13%
20%
BARF
39%

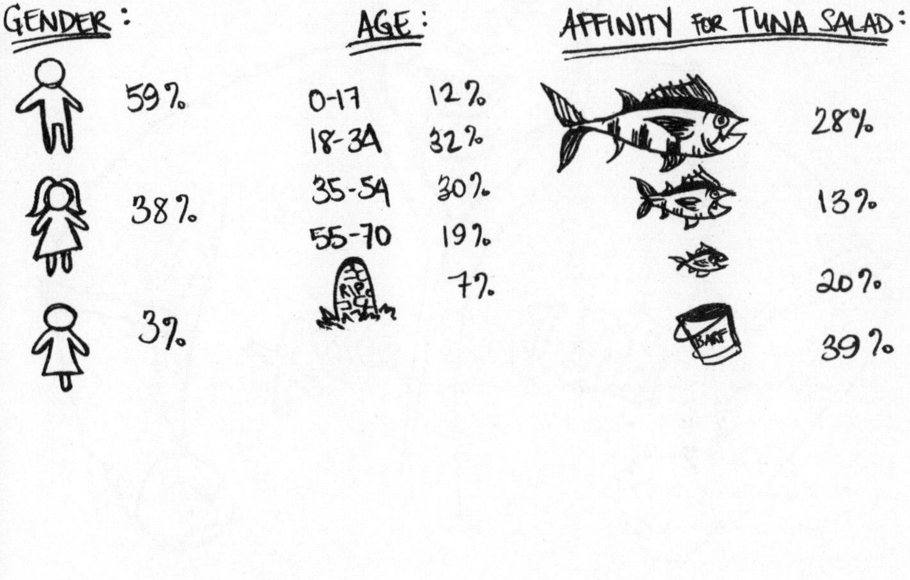

Some people need to learn to make up their mind—politicians, girlfriends, terrorists, et cetera. But none of these flip-flopping John Kerrys can hold an indecisive flame to Bandwagon Fan. Indentified by his blasé attitude toward any form of sports franchise for the entirety of the regular season, this Wagoner jumps on whatever team happens to be on top as soon as the playoffs begin.

No matter where the team is from or what sport they play, if the Poughkeepsie Pocket Knives are the team to beat, then BF is their biggest fan. And holy Don Shula, does it make us PMS-y. There you are, finally celebrating the rise of your Santa Barbara Shortcakes team, only to discover some jackass dressed in a full-blown angel-food-cake jumpsuit, proclaiming how "he's been a fan since Jesus was just a carpenter." Oh hell no, counterfeit cowboy, not on our watch. It doesn't matter how loud you cheer, or how many car flags you can fit on your Thunderbird, we know that when our team was locked in the cellar, you were slutting your support elsewhere.

Pick a team and stick with it, people: no trading, no changing sides because you picked the Buccaneers. Like the tattoo you got in Phuket, once you've made your decision, there is no going back. Don't make our fists switch allegiances between our wrists and your face.

OFFICE FANTASY FOOTBALL FREAK

Work alone is reason enough to bust out your medicine cabinet full of sleeping pills—unproductive meetings, excessive emoticons, slutty interns who refuse to sleep with you even after you offer to pay them in Guinean Francs. But none of these compares to the gadfly that is Office Fantasy Football Freak. Unfamiliar with societal norms and running low on Cymbalta, OFFF is spiraling into a bracket of darkness, and only accepting a miniature plaque at the end-of-season T.G.I. Friday's banquet can pull him out.

Looking for OFFF? Find him in the supply room, hunched behind his Acer between 9:00 and 4:45, pounding root beers and continually refreshing his customized Yahoo! page for the sign that your running back has busted his ACL. Then it's all "Trade you my golden ball carrier for a sunset ballroom dance lesson with your wife." We're all for a little healthy simulation, but the adulterous swapping has got to stop. OFFF may be peeved about his failed attempt to re-create the '76 Padres dynasty, but spitting in our tuna sandwich is crossing the line. Sorry Steve "Star Quarterback" screwed you over by sucking so hard, but take it out on your own blow-up doll, you shady in-house lawyer.

If your office has its very own mock sport sociopath, you may want to extend a bonus mid-year review. Sit him down in a professional manner, pin a steak to his face, and call your famous Statue of Liberty play (lit torch optional). Engagement is the cornerstone of a profitable work force.

SUPER SNORER

In 1848, John Wilkes Booth shared a bunk at fat camp with a kid who wore an unnecessary top hat and sleep-wheezed louder than a sedated Free Willy in a headgear. Seventeen years later, he went ape-shit on a balcony. Coincidence? You said it, not us.

Fellow humans, if there is one thing we all hold in equally high regard, it's the chance to escape our pitiful little lives for six dreamy hours every night in a three-way with Megan Fox and Guard #2 from *Robin Hood: Prince of Thieves*. Take that away from us and we have nothing but the Olive Garden's unlimited soup, salad, and breadstick combo to look forward to. And that only happens on special occasions. So you can imagine the Napoleonic rage that rises in our black hearts when Super Snorer goes into a 200-decibel coma just seconds before we doze off, leaving us to sit up all night memorizing the breathing patterns of an Afrin addict with sleep apnea and the farts.

This shit is serious. Sleep deprivation can lead to insanity, and insanity can lead to buying sweatshirts at Abercrombie. Needless to say, if someone you sleep next to is an SS, try performing your very own uvulopalatopharyngoplasty. If the surgery doesn't take, you can always try the holistic approach. Namely, sticking your fist so far down the snorer's throat, you can pump his lungs manually.

BAGGAGE FEES

By the time this book goes to print, the cost of checking your leopard-print Samsonite will most likely have risen to $100. By the time you finish this sentence, $200. And by the time you put this book down in favor for one about poo, airlines will probably be charging your unborn children for the luxury of going on the same trip as your Speedo. Man, we haven't seen a rip-off this big since the time we tried to buy an extra spleen in Chinatown.

The barbaric baggage business has got to stop. If we don't act soon, airplane seats will be collecting DNA samples while we sleep for their exclusive deal with Megacorp Novelty Mugs International. What gives you flying sky machines the right to make your service even shittier, only to have us cough up more money? There's no guarantee the plane will even stay in the air, but you're going to charge us an arm, a leg, and a liver just to bring our clean Hello Kitty underwear along for the ride? Blasphemy.

Failure to ground this type of behavior will result in incremental charges beyond belief. Soon we'll be paying for seat belts, wings, and the promise of sober pilots. So next time you board a baggage cart, make sure to land a couple to Wyoming Air's nose cone, free of charge.

HISTORY OF PEOPLE WHO DESERVE IT

A CHRONOLOGICAL ACCOUNT OF FAMOUS HOSERS SINCE THE BIG BANG.

Vlad "The Impaler" Dracula

Truth is, it's hard for us to hate on the guy who inspired *Bram Stoker's Dracula*, but as you can read, his nickname alludes to his love for shoving pointy stakes into innocent people's tooshies, so you can see our dilemma. Some say Vlad the Impaler was just getting revenge against the Ottoman douche lords who killed his pops. We say revenge is Sally Field packing a revolver in *Eye for an Eye*. And even though the original vampire was voted one of the 100 greatest Romanians, we still say he deserved a facial skinning, fangs and all.

Eve

Damn, girl, just had to go and give in to temptation, didn't you? And for what? An apple, please! We might be able to forgive you if an Xbox was dangling, but a piece of fruit? Nope. We've all been booted from paradise and forced to wear Banana Republic just so you could get some fiber? Eat a plant, bitch, you're in a garden! This original sin calls for a punch to the apple core. Ya heard?

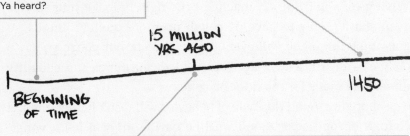

15 MILLION YRS AGO

BEGINNING OF TIME

1450

The AIDS Monkey

Monkeys are cute, funny, and can be trained to bring beer, so it's hard to hate. Unless of course said monkey brings you a side of HIV with your brewski. Damn AIDS Monkey. You killed the party without even a sense of irony. As soon as we track down Dustin Hoffman and his fancy yellow suit we are going to launch an outbreak on your ass. Right after we find out what exactly happened in *I Heart Huckabees*.

Nathan Bedford Forrest

While the true father of the Ku Klux Klan remains unknown, we can tell you that Nathan Bedford Forrest became the Klan's first Grand Wizard (sun-and-moon cone hats were vetoed upon suggestion). Mr. Bedford Forrest, not only do you hide under the sheets like a girl, but your spry 'stache makes you look like a Dungeons & Dragons reject. Sheeeet, with that kind of notoriety we don't even have to knock you out. We might suggest a comb-over though.

1852

1861

Boss Tweed

If you thought Madoff was a steaming pile of aardvark shite, better get acquainted with Tweed, the New York senator who straight up stole taxpayers' money—without the pansy cover-up. Nope, boss man preferred to just add some zeros to the government checks and cash the suckers himself, like Diddy at the annual Bad Boy shareholders meeting. Dude bamboozled like $40 million in 1870s dollars. Adjusting for inflation, that's like settling a divorce with Tiger Woods. Twice.

John Wayne Gacy

If ever there was an argument to be made for clown genocide, this guy is it. Sure, he gave the "no feeling" to a couple of young'uns before he became "Pogo the Clown," but John Wayne Gacy, the KFC manager, local activist, contractor, and serial killer, did most of his damage after giving himself the white-face makeover. During his reign of terror, Krusty raped and murdered at least 33 boys and young men, leaving them to decompose in a crawl space under his basement. Also an argument for finished basements.

1971

1977

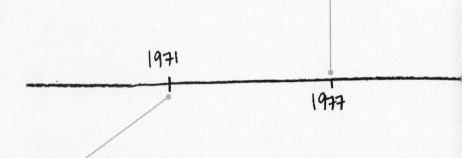

Idi Amin

Oh, Idi, you put the crazy in crazy, know what Amin? First, you go and rename yourself "His Excellency, President for Life, Field Marshal . . . Conqueror of the British Empire in Africa in General and Uganda in Particular." Then, you go and clog the Ugandan hydroelectric dam with 500,000 bodies. And as if that weren't nasty enough, you make a meal out of it. Way to package the seven sins, glutton murderer!

Tonya Harding

Satan, the Chicago Cubs, Tiger Woods—all amazing sore losers. Still, none compares to Miss Tonya Harding. Tired of continually getting her ass handed to her by Nancy Kerrigan, America's sweetheart and pre-YouPorn fantasy, Old Tea Bag Tonya decided to level the playing field one kneecap at a time. This greasy ponytail might not have done the crow bashing, but in the court of PWDI, being named Tonya is nine-tenths of the law, and the verdict is two 9.0s to the double axel.

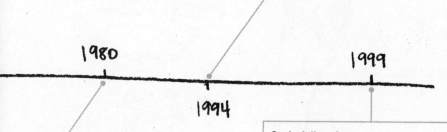

1980

1999

1994

Mark David Chapman

As if gunning down one of the greatest musicians of our time wasn't bad enough, Mark David Chapman solidified his spot as the #1 Worst-Dressed Assassin on the Planet. Way to go, Mark. Not only is December 4, 1980, the day the music died, but it's also the day the world decided to treat America like the Norman Bates of the universe. Happiness may be a warm gun to John, but to us it's a lukewarm fist to your four eyes.

Dr. Jack Kevorkian

Let's clear something up right now: Dr. K isn't on this list because we agree or disagree with euthanasia. To each his own. Sometimes when reflecting on that spring night of '92 in the Nanking Buffet parking lot, we too succumb to dark thoughts. The Kevorkster is on notice because he vaulted himself into the spotlight by notching a couple assists in the suicide stat book. To see the instant replays, please visit YouDied.fakeurl. Yes, DK became a household name just like Bill Cosby, but instead of hawking Jell-O, Doc was peddling D-e-a-t-h-O.

CONTINUOUS SPORTS METAPHOR DUDE

Much like Malaysian Easy Mac with ponzu sauce, when it comes to sports metaphors, a little goes a long way. So when Continuous Sports Metaphor Dude starts throwing them out like beads at the Bead Factory Mardi Gras party, it feels a lot like being trapped between Coach K's ass cheeks after an all-you-can-eat shrimp scampi buffet.

Our beef is not so much with the occasional sports colloquialism seasoning the water cooler. In fact, we've even been known to throw around a "hole-in-one" in our day. But to assist it with an "out-of-the-park home run, slam-dunk mulligan, in the bottom of the ninth, fourth quarter" in one 30-minute meeting, activates our homicidal tic faster than OJ driving by a Bronco dealership.

Even though Obama is dropping athletic allegories quicker than he can spend a zillion dollars, there is still no excuse for Continuous Sports Metaphor Dude to violate our ear cavities. So, the next time he tries to equate our 3 p.m. status meeting to the 1976 World Series, you'd better believe we're putting him down for the count. Damn it, we did it again.

Since the dawn of man, poor, innocent un-crackers have been discriminated against for their skin pigments and adorable foreign accents. This cannot be denied. But in this day and age, with interracial cereal box covers like Good Friends by Kashi, it's hard to believe every injustice is directly attributable to the thickness of someone's hair.

Not so for Everything's Racist Guy, the delusional nut job who accuses the bagel guy of being a hooded knight when Bruegger's runs out of low-fat chive. Even Malcolm X knew that sometimes the cream cheese inventory runs low. Time to learn it's not always the color of your inner thigh that determines how Walgreens treats you—sometimes its just luck of the draw or the fact that your legs are bleeding.

Next time you overhear ERG filing a wrongful dismissal claim, quickly remind him that his firing had nothing to do with his yarmulke and everything to do with his centaur-porn addiction, then give him a real reason to sue. And by that, we mean make sure you have a lawyer before you take affirmative action.

Every day, millions of illegal immigrants smuggle themselves in the linings of Ford Pintos for the chance to spit in the streets unpunished and realize their dreams of becoming American supermarket tycoons. Yet here we have a flesh-and-blood gringo behind the conveyor belt, pissing away the American dream and treating our groceries like dime-store hookers after a night on Capitol Hill: swipe, pass, and pile.

Shame on you, Bad Bagger. Did you learn nothing from your privileged upbringing on Tetris and Dr. Mario? Have you no respect for the fragility of the quail egg? Do you know how long it takes one of those teeny chickens to push a speckled beauty out of its miniature vajazzle? Clearly not. If you did, you wouldn't toss it in the bag like a used sheepskin after a night of Tomato-Nutella sandwiches and World of Warcraft code breaking.

If we ever find our vine tomatoes pinned beneath the Tropicana, we're going to bag you. In the face. And not with that breathable canvas shit you're selling the hippie kids for $5 a pop.

PEOPLE WHO DON'T DESERVE IT

For every one million assholes exists a
baby Jesus who deserves a Fruit Roll-Up.

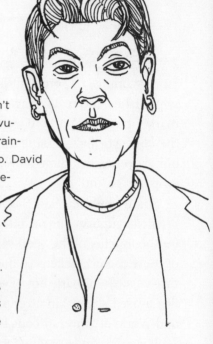

BRIAN AUSTIN GREEN

Is there a post-pubescent boy who wouldn't
want to occupy this guy's shoes, or an ovulating tween who wouldn't unclasp her training bra in his presence? The answer is no. David
Silver not only dominated the seminal television show of the past 3,000 years,
but also every beauty this side of
Bollywood. Brian Austin Green is a
sexy time bomb sent back in time for
more sex. Don Green Juan is unstoppable.
Megan Fox was all, "I want to marry you,
B," and he was like, "Maybe," and she was
like, "Cool." Only B.A.G. would stand at the
pearly vajayjays and ask for a taste test.

We salute you, Greenie. Not only did you give us one of the greatest underage television coke-addicts of our generation, but you proved that even
a D-list celebrity can still get grade A ass. Slow clap . . .

FAVORITE PRESSURE POINT

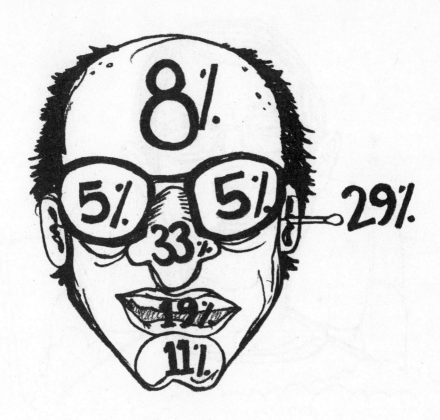

AUTOMOBILE ASS DROPPER

Road trips are great. The open road in front of you, the wind at your back, and four of your best friends stuffed in a '96 Honda Accord. Yes, this is the stuff of legends. Unfortunately for you, the amigo in your passenger seat is none other than the infamous Automobile Ass Dropper, armed with a cannon for a colon and an affinity for air defecating the second you hit the turnpike.

Just like that, your tale of trans-American travel goes from Hardy Boys to Garbage Pail Kids in a single second. All you're left with is a burning sensation in your sinus, false accusations, and a Japanese shit sauna doing 55 down the freeway. And with the number of Flying Js, Travel Americas, and Road Kill Shake Shacks littering the off-ramps, AAD has enough fuel to power his rectal rocket from Minnesota to the moon.

Stopped to fill up and discovered Automobile Ass Dropper topping up on chili dogs? Fear not, there's a way to get your bromance wagon back on track. Simply remind him gas goes in the car, not out his tailpipe, with a couple shots to the grill.

FROSTBITE

Weather is like an ovulating transsexual: one minute she's hot and horny and the next he's the ice queen of Quebec City. Only it's worse, because giving the weather a horse tranquilizer has virtually no effect at all. Instead, we are forced inside our homes to fraternize with family members, lest we risk suffering Mama Nature's wrath. And for some reason, losing our thumbs to Uncle Eddie's cannibalism seems more excruciating than exposing our baby-soft skin to the wretched elements.

So, we brave it. But we made a mistake. The winds pick up and eat our flesh more brutally than a termite field trip to a marionette factory. Our fingers, they bleed on the inside, and then they die. Frostbite murders them. And gets off every time. Just like Zsa Zsa Gabor.

Oh, the injustice. Damn you, Frostbite! Damn your slow infliction and numbing pain and pussy-ass excuse to hit the ski chalet. If we ever come face-to-face with you again, we're going to use what remains of our limbs to rub hot chilies in your eye. We hope you melt to death in a pool of your own ice shards.

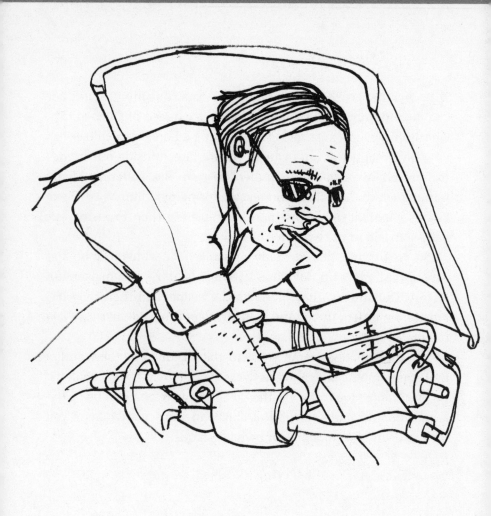

CROOKED CAR MECHANIC

Ever since Henry Ford pushed that first Model T out of his prostate, automobiles have been falling apart exactly six minutes after the factory warranty expires. It's as much a part of the car-owning experience as getting laid in the back seat, ghost riding the whip, and driving blitzed on 12 Zimas.

DUI or not, however, one should never be forced to cope with the physical, mental, and financial exploitation that is a trip to the Crooked Car Mechanic. Identified from miles away by his used Norma Rae overalls and his shiny rapist glow, CCM sets about siphoning your penny jar the minute your jalopy pulls onto the lot. Everything starts off peachy: He's "happy to take a look," and, "oh sure, fixing that won't be a problem," but before you know it, that low tire pressure has turned into a broken axle, a split carburetor, and a mean case of shingles. Yeah, you could take it for a second opinion, but your '92 Saab is already up on the rig with five of its wheels missing. What's a brother to do but vomit $9,200?

Okay, fine, choosing a life in the performing arts and being confused by the word "engine" qualifies you for a hot tire-ironing, but in twenty-first-century Metro USA, nobody should be ostracized for their daintiness unless they're on *American Idol*. So when CCM tries to fleece you out of house and home, try picking up a wrench (it's the claw-like one) and knocking the blue right out of his collar.

LOSER WHO LAMENTS ABOUT TURNING 25

Oh man, life is tough. There are electric bills to pay, global warming to refute, and we still don't know how many licks it takes to get to the center of a Tootsie Pop. But for Loser Who Laments About Turning 25, all is trumped by the impending halfway-to-50 mark.

Soaking up the tears with the wads of disposable income that come with a full-time job and no dependents, LWLATT grieves for lost youth. Gone are the good old days of soiling yourself and burying mom's Prozac in the sandbox, and here to stay are the horrendously defined six-packs and outrageous feelings of entitlement. Oh, woe is you, Lamenting Loser; it must be hard watching your body recover immediately from a night of binge drinking. We're sorry to hear about your impending six-month self-discovery tour of Thailand and subsequent seven-figure book deal. Can we offer you a designer handkerchief to wipe away your pH-balanced bodily fluids?

Should you run into this sad clown crying over 26 diamond birthday candles (one for good luck!), kindly remind him some people have real problems, one face punch at a time.

PEOPLE
WHO DESERVE IT
THROUGH TIME
Eventually, someone will invent a time machine. So get ready because
the past and the future are equally littered with heinousness.

B ack in the 1960s, when George Jetson hired Rosie (the robot cleaning lady) to wash his space suits and vacuum the flying Pinto, he didn't envision her talking back after requesting a rub and tug at the end of a long day.

Fast-forward 82 years and all of a sudden our man-made aluminum slaves are passing moral judgment left and right. You don't even have a heart, Tin Man, so how can you pass judgment on our new crude oil dumping hobby? Last time we checked, you're nothing more than a microwave with legs. We steal one Uranus Gold Bar from the hologram bodega and all of a sudden you're Mother Teresa. This ain't computing.

We dare you to refuse to sell us a six-pack of Lunar Madness because we don't have our DNA chips. You may have eye sockets, but only because we gave them to you. And we can just as easily take them back. Uh . . . fill them up.

NO UMBRELLA ETIQUETTE LADY

You know this bitch. She comes out in the rain. Flourishes in it, actually. Because evaporated water falling from the sky is her green light to start impaling innocent eyeballs on the street with her giant parasol, like Shaquille O'Neal swinging his jimmy obliviously in the streets of Shanghai.

The original menace to society, No Umbrella Etiquette Lady thrusts through crowds with absolutely no regard for the umbrella-yielding code. There's no lifting for oncoming traffic, no lowering for the abnormally tall—just straight up eye harvesting. And all under the safe haven of her '74 PGA poke stick.

Connecting with NUEL's face can be tough, given her protective shield, so you'll need to get creative. Whatever method of punishment you choose, just make sure you let it rain.

FAKE FAILURE

Sometimes life deals you a rough hand and there's nothing you can do about it. It's not Rumer Willis's fault she looks like a potato. But what can she do? We'll tell you what: She can take her rage out on Fake Failure, the perfect human specimen who promises she "fully bombed" her interview, only to be hired on as President of the Solar System.

Chances are you first met this wolf-crying compliment-fisher sometime in grade school, when her standard response to any post-pop-quiz difficulty survey was, "Oh my god, I totally failed. Kill me now." Only the bitch never failed. She got 92 percent every goddamn time, while the rest of us got papers resembling a Quentin Tarantino screenplay after going through the ringer at Disney.

If it's praise she's after, give Fake Failure what she wants. Butter her up like a 16-pound turkey on Thanksgiving Day. Get that shit in all the creases, oil her thighs with adulation and then, right before she starts to brown, stuff your fist so far up that the giblets fly out of her mouth.

What's the capital of Ecuador? How many mammals are indigenous to Guam? What is the square root of 646? Don't know? That's okay, because we know someone who will be happier than a lizard at a flea convention to tell you the answer. That is, right after he recounts how he spent the last six months learning Sanskrit, studying planetary creation, and rewriting the United Nations charter.

Ladies and gentlemen, brothers and sisters, Internet freaks, we introduce to you Mr. Know-It-All, who thinks the road to popularity is paved with the ability to answer any question, even if wasn't asked of him. Interested in knowing that the gross domestic product of Taiwan is $698.6 billion, or that hops are female flowers? No? Doesn't matter, because if your conversation is anywhere near the vicinity of MKIA, he's going to be replacing your "who" with "whom" faster than a mathlete regrows his virginity.

Of course, being s-m-r-t is totally r-a-d. It's just that when MKIA starts making our brain freeze with Peruvian mortality stats, we start to feel like we did in the sixth grade—dumb, lost, and angry on the inside. Nothing a couple of shots to the knowledge factory couldn't put an end to.

OBVIOUSLY HOT COMPLIMENT FISHER

Oh my god! I am sooooo fugly. I'm like a total heifer. My cuticles are gross, my hairline is beat, my pores are disgusting, and my vastus medialis is completely bloated. I am Obviously Hot Compliment Fisher!

Fuck, lady, you're gorgeous, okay? You know it, we know it, even Stevie Wonder knows it. So how about you lay off the false self-deprecation, Barbie, because we're on to you like a constipated sailor to a marine laxative sale. Not only do your vaguely concealed pleas for kudos insult our intelligence; they're offensive. Gross cuticles aren't something to joke about; they're disgusting, chapped, and hurt in the winter. Believe us—we know from experience.

So instead of your annoying unwillingness to admit your boobs are hot, how about you shut your perfectly proportioned jawline right this second. Because if you don't, we're going to give our vocal cords a rest and let our fists do the complimenting.

CHECKOUT ITEM FORGETTER

Lots of situations call for high fives—getting two candy bars from the vending machine when you only pay for one, finding money in your pocket, not being pregnant—but getting stuck in line behind Checkout Item Forgetter is not one of them. In fact, this scenario calls for something entirely different, and it involves using the tube socks you haven't purchased yet to build a makeshift coin weapon.

Unfamiliar with the concept of list making, Checkout Item Forgetter spends 45 minutes perusing the aisles of Walgreens for nothing in particular, filling her basket with wondrous products she has no use for, then waiting until all the Rogaine and eyelash moisturizer has been rung up to realize she didn't get the eau de bacon. Don't worry, CIF, we'll just wait here and stare awkwardly at the vacant cashier, hoping he'll let us pay for our Pomegranate Lip Smackers before you get back with your pork perfume.

Actually, you should worry. Because we have a flesh-and-blood eHarmony meet 'n' greet in 15 minutes and if we don't have super shiny lips when the curtain rises, our one chance at sex this year will be lost and it'll all be your fault. So while you're back in aisle six looking for the floss, better check out the deals on ice packs for your future broke face.

PEOPLE WHO
DON'T
DESERVE IT

For every one million assholes exists a
baby Jesus who deserves a Fruit Roll-Up.

GHOSTS

Paranormal activity is so hot right now.
But the truth is, fragile, squeamish
living beings have been taking out
their irrational fears on innocent
spirits of the afterlife for hundreds
of years. Scrooge, Hamlet, Dan Aykroyd—
all tormenters of airy non-people. And for
what? Is a wispy floating remnant of Pat-
rick Swayze really threatening enough to
merit the rash of a proton gun? Don't be
a hater.

The undead suffered enough during the
living part of life, what with its poison ivy,
Haley Joel Osment movies, and trans fats.
Who are we to put a stitch in their haunting?
Just because we can't yet absorb into the walls
of a David Barton Gym locker room is no reason for
us to jealously punish lingering auras. So here's to
you, ghosts. May you continue to blaze a trail of nasty
green goo longer than Slimer.

WORST HOLIDAY OFFENDER

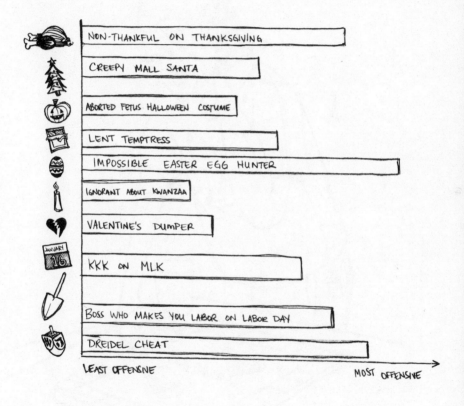

NON-THANKFUL ON THANKSGIVING

CREEPY MALL SANTA

ABORTED FETUS HALLOWEEN COSTUME

LENT TEMPTRESS

IMPOSSIBLE EASTER EGG HUNTER

IGNORANT ABOUT KWANZAA

VALENTINE'S DUMPER

KKK ON MLK

BOSS WHO MAKES YOU LABOR ON LABOR DAY

DREIDEL CHEAT

LEAST OFFENSIVE   MOST OFFENSIVE

DUDE WHO TAKES BOARD GAMES TOO SERIOUSLY

When it comes to board games, some friendly competition goes a long way. Keeps things interesting. But then there are those who treat every game like a death match with Dolph Lundgren, taking an exciting game of chance and turning it into the most excruciating three hours of your life since *The Postman* was in theaters.

It's times like these when you need to step back, take a deep breath, and remind Dude Who Takes Board Games Too Seriously to chill the fuck out before you break him off a piece of the Sorry board. After all, these are pastimes involving fake money, plastic properties, miniature hats, freehand drawing, and the ability to look like a fat man walking across coals. There will be no casualties if you accidentally land on Pennsylvania Avenue.

Instead of going all ten-year-old in a Yoo-hoo withdrawal, threatening to unparticipate if you don't get to play banker, how about you pull up your diapers, temper that tantrum, and roll the dice. Don't make us crack open your community chest.

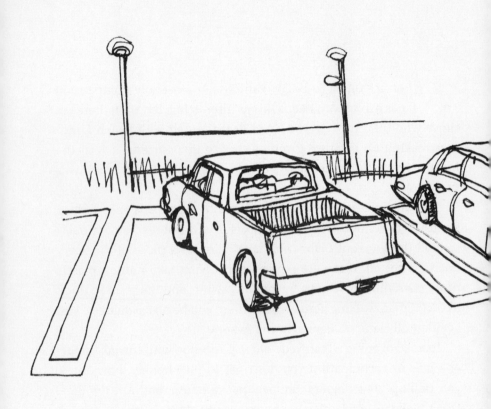

TWO-SPOT PARKER

America is a nation built on ideals: freedom of speech, freedom of the press, and freedom of assembly. This, however, does not give folks the right to park their PT Cruisers wherever they can fit the bumper. Regardless of how close you'd like to be to Long John Silver's, your proximity to deep-fried sea gruel is not protected under the constitution.

Yet every day across this great land, Two-Spot Parker treats the mall parking lot like it was constructed in his honor. We ain't at the trailer park, boyee, and your moves are upsetting us to the point of soiling our Depends. Damn it, TSP, those lines were put there for a reason—to ensure as many people as possible can get discount socks, ab crunchers, and giant pretzels under one roof. To fuck with the parking lines is to fuck with the U S of A, and that is going to get you an eagle talon to the tail pipe. *Kawwww.*

Should you pull into the Brandmart to find Two-Spot Parker hogging all the real estate, do your patriotic duty and explain that it's not the car he should worry about denting, it's his forehead.

OFFICE FOOD THIEF

You know what sucks about bringing your lunch to work (other than making it the night before, suffering the ridicule of co-workers, and washing out the Tupperware in the co-ed bathroom when you're done)? Having your mayo masterpiece stolen by Office Food Thief.

Oh, you know who you are, stealer of sustenance; sneaking into the break room just before noon to peruse the menu of bagged delicacies. Ooh! Turkey and Swiss on rye with a side of couscous . . . doesn't that sound delicious? Or maybe you'll go with the leftover shepherd's pie. So many choices, so little morals. Even in the back alleys of Beirut, where the chicken salad is bountiful and the laws are not, there still exists a code of honor among the cats and outlaws: If it ain't yours, don't lick it.

Guess what, Thiefy? The name on the top of that yogurt? Not arbitrary! So get your filthy hands off our brown bags, or it's gonna be Knuckle-Sandwich Monday every day this week. Ten punches and you get one free.

Ever wonder how the guy across from you at work has lived in the Congo, fought with the African militia, been a CIA spy, climbed Everest in two hours, made love to a Swedish princess in a dragon's lair, and managed to learn Microsoft Excel in the same lifetime? Us too. That is, until we wised up to the scent of his pants on fire. Sorry to kill your faith in humanity, but your cubicle comrade is Compulsive Liar.

Hey now. We love a good story; *Battlestar Galactica* all the way. But at a certain point a man goes too far. Why lie about your dog's pedigree? Even if you were telling the truth about him being half lab, half Norwegian mountain goat, it wouldn't matter. Who exactly are you trying to impress? We don't care if you are a direct descendent of Moses, or that you can put 65 Ping-Pong balls in your mouth. Come to think of it, we're pretty sure you didn't drink 72 liters of vodka last night, because you'd be dead, and frankly, that wouldn't have been the worst thing.

Sorry, that was excessive. Really though, next time you go Pinocchio on our asses, we are going to clog your lie-hole with a righteous handful of truth-fist.

Salami. It's mysterious and delicious. That's why we eat it and don't ask silly questions, like "What's this stuff made of?" or, "Does my right eyeball look loose to you?" It's also why we keep our mouths closed when it comes back up two hours later in the form of a nuclear gas bomb that, if released, could exterminate all of South Korea with one whiff. (Two for North.) Unfortunately not everyone graduates cum laude from the New Jersey State Charm School. Some choose to live a life of vile mouth flatulence. And by some, we mean Stink Burper.

After a three-tzatziki-martini lunch, nothing amuses this grease bag more than unleashing a mustard gas cloud on a group of unsuspecting breathers. Some thoughts going through your mind right now may be "Ack!" and "Why doesn't the beast cover his stink hole?!" Both are common reactions to such an offense. Truth is, Stink Burper doesn't have enough brain capacity after downing a 19-pound Slim Jim to coordinate the cover-up.

If you ever come into contact with people who masticate, chances are said oxygen-soiler will rear his stink waves in an enclosed space sometime soon. But fear not. If the ancient Mongolian garlic farmers taught us anything, it's the stink-burp oppression technique: look for the two-second suck-in warning sign, throw a left hook, and watch the salami smoke billow into someone else's nostrils.

PEOPLE WHO
DON'T
DESERVE IT

For every one million assholes exists a
baby Jesus who deserves a Fruit Roll-Up.

WHOEVER INVENTED DUNKAROOS

Exotic game is one of life's rare treats: antelope, bison, chipmunk embryo—all attractive breakfast options. But none beat the succulent delight of a wild kangaroo wearing a cute hat dunked in a vat of creamy high-fructose corn syrup, served in a pocket-size snacking device.

Dang, cartoon marsupial, that shit is good. Whoever took the leftover brown acid from the "Woodstock Memories" box they found in the garage and concocted this recipe deserves a cinnamon cookie scalp massage, even if they haven't produced a fresh pack since Kirstie Alley fit on one TV screen.

As long as condemned dollar stores keep reorganizing snacks from 1988 so they can rent out their stock rooms to Libyan refugees, we will keep purchasing these tiny boxes of processed crack. So thank you, mystery human being, for solving world hunger. And by "world" we mean us, at 5 a.m., after downing a six-pack of Smirnoff Ice and watching a *California Dreams* marathon.

PERSON WHO MOST DESERVES IT AT SUMMER CAMP

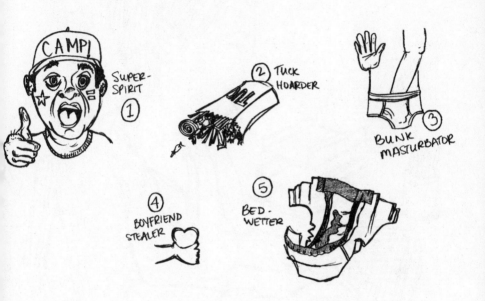

1 SUPER-SPIRIT

2 TUCK HOARDER

3 BUNK MASTURBATOR

4 BOYFRIEND STEALER

5 BED-WETTER

Sorry team, you'll be working late again tonight :)

Looks like we're gonna have to let you go :p

Oops, I ran over your cat :o

Do any of these statements make you feel good? No, they don't. In fact, they probably make you want rip out all your hair, get a Bosley hair treatment, and rip it out all over again. So why, then, does Passive Aggressive Emoticon User feel the need to end each suffocating thought with a rage-inducing smiley face? Or worse, a wink?

We'll tell you why. Because she's a horrible ingrate who takes pleasure in other people's misery. Or her life could be so loveless, this is a desperate attempt and cry for—Nah . . . girl's a bitch. Should you have your very own PAEU, remind her that projecting her pathological disorder on others is unacceptable by replying to her next email with your own emoticon. What's the symbol for hanging jawbone again?

When the Cold War ended, millions of young Americans who had no idea it was going on in the first place felt the need to celebrate with a special commemorative hairstyle. So they went on the new interspatial World Wide Web and searched Lycos for "awesome looks from the future." What resulted was a plague so strong it morphed the very fabric of our DNA to create Frosted Tips Bro.

Like a porcupine with a vengeance problem, Frosted Tips Bro will take your eye out with a hair spike so bleached it will burn through your cornea and disintegrate your black heart. Listen, Dye Job, we know b4-4 was the seminal boy band in your life, but unless you're an LA Dodger teleported to present day with extra-tight spandex and a Swarovski jockstrap, there's no reason for this assault on mankind's ego. We have *The Bachelor* for that.

Retribution for this douchely offense comes in many forms, but our personal favorite is the Mohel. Gather some friends, say a prayer, and snip those tips. And if Spencer Pratt resists, rock him to sleep. With a real rock. Then it's bagel time! Mazel tov.

SLOW WALKER SIDEWALK BLOCKER

Hmm. Lovely day for a stroll, isn't it, Slow Walker Sidewalk Blocker? Maybe a little meandering in the park? A leisurely promenade by the river? A jaunt in the middle of a crowded street, where people actually have shit to do and are forced to suffer as you take in the sights at the pace of a newborn deer?

Everybody hates you.

You clog our sidewalks and subway platforms. You make us late and irritable. You ruin the morning before the day even starts. Whoever let you out of the puzzle factory should be subjected to alien brain experiments. At this glacial pace you'll never make it to the DIY dental clinic anyway, so why even bother? How about you do us all a favor and stay indoors with your stray cat collection and stop clogging our route to the 99-cent midget peep show. Keep it up and one of these days you will get punched in the face. And it will be nobody's fault but your own.

EIGHT-MINUTE VOICEMAIL LEAVER

Beep. "Hey, buddy, it's me. Listen, I was thinking about that thing we were talking about last night and you were totally right. I should stop fantasizing about your mom. It's effed up. She doesn't even look that hot in her Levi's. I just said that to piss you off. And her cooking kind of sucks. Who wants to bang a MILF who can't bake? Plus, your dad's been all up in there, and it grosses me out a little. Anyway, yeah. Just wanted to let you know. We should hang this weekend. I hear that tanning salon on Palmerson is throwing a luau. You still have that sunscreen from Burning Man, right? Call me." *Beep.*

Like the rough hand of an Estonian bookie, Eight-Minute Voice-mail Leaver makes you wait through the pain before you can even think of erasing the memories. Try as you may to delete the diatribe, failure is imminent. You press 1, it restarts. You press #, it translates to Bulgarian. You press 5, it sends the sound waves to your brain and plays on repeat for eternity (new feature).

Well, guess what, Eight-Minute Voicemail Leaver? We don't have the time or the patience to sit through 480 seconds of pocket-dialing from naked bingo night at the planetarium. So either give us the crib notes on your night in Talladega, or risk getting *69ed to the face—in a totally nonsexual but still physically uncomfortable way.

BITCH WHO TALKS ON CELL PHONE AT HOLOCAUST MUSEUM

Wow! This bitch cannot stand being out of touch. She could be mid-labor with an 18-pound future Baltimore Ravens linebacker blitzing his way out of her wah-wah and she'd still take a call.

Seriously, lady, what could possibly be so important that you have to pick up in front of the Children's Bones display case? You ain't Pol Pot, and the world isn't going to implode if you can't get to your Sidekick. Okay, fine, New Jersey might implode, but it's on its way already. Even Zack Morris laid off the three-million-pound Motorola when he took the tour. It's a matter of respect. Like burping in the chef's face when you eat in Japan. Or is it China? Better not take our word for it.

Lucky for us, spotting Bitch Who Talks on Cell Phone at Holocaust Museum is easier than finding a giant needle in a tiny haystack. First you'll notice the ingrate rifling through her purse for the infamous phone. Next comes the brutally long Usher ringtone, followed by the split second of contemplation before deeming the call "urgent."

If caught at either of these stages, a preemptive punch is in order. If forced to endure any number of "oh my gods," "no ways," or "shut ups!"—punch harder.

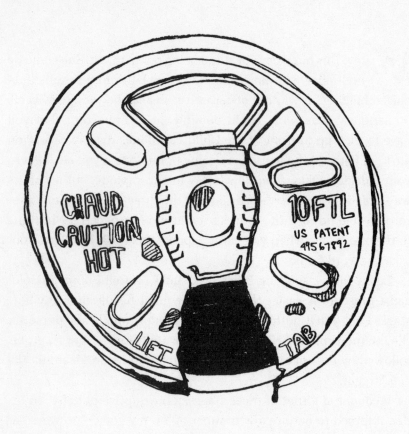

FAULTY COFFEE LID

While technically not a person, Faulty Coffee Lid is definitely up there with the all-time offenders. In human form, FCL most resembles an 18-year-old backpacker with dengue fever and a bad case of the butterfingers. It's amazing how something with such a basic job can fail so miserably.

There you are, enjoying a double hot, no-foam, soy chai, extra caramel, kitty-litter latte, cruising down I-95, busting out to Men at Work, when all of a sudden you feel the hot rattle of a lid trying to escape. Before you know it, there's $80 worth of scalding-hot liquid running down your neck, and the cashmere mock turtleneck you purchased is as soiled as the inside of a summer camp sleeping bag.

Enough is enough. Next time you trick us into thinking you've got our back, you'd better watch out, because the fists you're about to receive are marked "extremely hot."

INCESSANT INTERRUPTER

When our forefathers sat down to pen the First Amendment, those wig-wearing white guys could not have imagined the chaos that would accompany giving everyone the right to say whatever shit came to mind. Now, 6,000 years later, we're left with crazy talk of alien landings, racist revolutions, and *The View*. But worse than all of cable's soapboxes put together is the person who can't even wait for your sentence to finish before cutting you off like a cabby during switchover.

Her name: Incessant Interrupter. Her purpose: to make sure you never complete another sentence in your entire life. What does Incessant Interrupter have to say that is so important it warrants dismissing your story about murderous coconuts? It doesn't matter. Your voice is occupying her speaking space, and Little Miss Can't Wait Her Turn dominates her territory like a Canadian while curling. Oh, you'll get to finish your closing argument, but only after she wastes every last lung pump explaining how she invented the teen vampire category.

Holy Louis Black, we hate you, Incessant Interrupter, you are probably trying to interrupt this as we type, aren't you? You know what? Why don't you just fill in the blanks: Next time we find you _____ we are going to _____ right in the _____ and _____ straight out to _____ until you end up with a _____ welt on your _____ _____!

INTERNATIONAL PEOPLE WHO DESERVE IT

DEGENERACY DOESN'T DISCRIMINATE.

Seal Clubber (Canada)

"Oh, Canada," home to universal health care, same-sex marriage, and the Barenaked Ladies. If a more liberal place existed, Howard Dean would be viceroy. So how the WWF did seal clubbing schmooze itself into becoming a national Canuck pastime? Bear or Bryan Adams clubbing, we could understand, but seals? Tabarnak, Canada! At least Americans kill things that can fight back, like eagles, dinosaurs, and people. Sad thing is, if you had decided to play Whack-A-Mole with say, Céline Dion, everything would be kosher. Unfortunately, we're forced to unilaterally fist break the 49th parallel, and we ain't even stopping at duty-free.

Organ Stealer (Colombia)

Traveling through Colombia is stressful enough, what with the dirt-cheap yayo and subsequent paranoia that Juan Valdez is trying to kill you in a government-sanctioned, Starbucks-funded java conspiracy. Then, to put the cherry on the Charlie, we gotta worry about Organ Stealer, the cash-strapped *taladro* who needs your pancreas to pay back the bookie he owes three zillion pesos for losing that bet on when Shakira's hips would start lying. Sheeeet, *hermano*. We could have told you the answer to that. It would have saved you all that bone sawing and kept our ability to break down carbs.

If you ever fall asleep beside a beautiful Colombian only to hear the door swing open, followed by the sound of a machete, put your dime bag to good use by giving the amateur surgeon *una cara nueva*.

Tap Water (Mexico)

If there are two things we know about Mexico, it's that the dogs are sick and the nightwalkers are cheap. Okay, three things. The water is poisoned with the rage of Montezuma, and his anger will haunt you like Bea Arthur's spirit at a weekend claims-adjuster convention. Damn you, Mexican Tap Water. All we wanted was six all-inclusive nights of underage foam-party fondling. But no. We can't decide if we're puking because we had a tap water drinking contest or because we're pregnant with a spring breaker's baby. So, the next time you attempt to hijack our colon like a straight-to-DVD Keanu Reeves movie, we're going to one-up you with a little thing we like to called iodine, sucka. Just as soon as we can stand without shitting our pants.

Sketchy Plastic Surgeon (Brazil)

With the increasing number of people getting work done these days, it's safe to say that 30 years from now, a good portion of the Western world will look like Jabba the Hut crawling out of a microwave. Especially those suckers who figured they'd save a couple extra shillings by visiting Sketchy Plastic Surgeon. Predictably, what they saved in money, they made up with in extra fish appendages, but what can you expect when your MD thinks the Hippocratic oath is a pledge you recite to hippopotamuses? When you finally wake from the roofie and find your ass crack lifted to your face, your best bet is to manually graft a fist to SPS's face until desired MJ resemblance is achieved.

Malaria Mosquitoes (Africa)

World travelers, meet Malaria Mosquito, the poor man's Robert Pattinson (Tom Cruise, for all you oldies) who sucks your blood without so much as a hint of sexual ambiguity, all in exchange for a life-threatening disease that doesn't bring you any closer to banging Anna Paquin. Yeah, yeah, we know what you're thinking: use a mosquito net, take your Malarone. But guess what? Mosquito nets are hot as ass wax and Malarone gives you nightmares about playing Scrabble with your boss in Kathleen Turner's body (check the label).

Should you find yourself face-to-face with the flying plague, take a cue from *Cops* and OFF a brother in the mosquito eye. With a thousand pupils, aim is overrated.

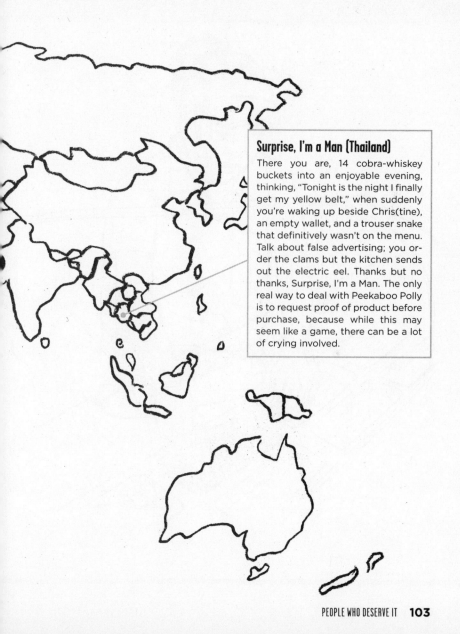

Surprise, I'm a Man (Thailand)

There you are, 14 cobra-whiskey buckets into an enjoyable evening, thinking, "Tonight is the night I finally get my yellow belt," when suddenly you're waking up beside Chris(tine), an empty wallet, and a trouser snake that definitely wasn't on the menu. Talk about false advertising; you order the clams but the kitchen sends out the electric eel. Thanks but no thanks, Surprise, I'm a Man. The only real way to deal with Peekaboo Polly is to request proof of product before purchase, because while this may seem like a game, there can be a lot of crying involved.

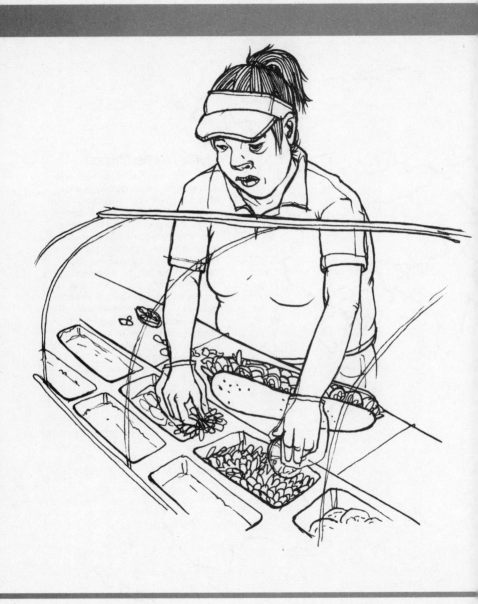

SLOPPY SANDWICH MAKER

There are only two things to look forward to during the work-day: lunch, and it no longer being the workday. So when some latex-clad, salami-yielding jerkstore screws with one of these little pleasures, shit gets serious.

Seriously, Sloppy Sandwich Maker? You're gonna squirt all the mayo on the right side of the ciabatta and leave the turkey in a clumped-up heap on the left? Great. That will go perfectly with the semi-toasted bread you ran through the toaster for 2.3 seconds and the chopped onions you hid in the darkest corners of your concoction, even after we asked for no onions. Twice.

Holy black forest ham, we hate you, SSM. Not only for ruining what could have been the best 12 minutes of our day, but for disgracing your sandwich-making peers who respect the responsibility that comes with crafting a well-balanced meal. Next time we catch you putting pickles where they shouldn't be, you might want to make sure you're nowhere near the meat slicer.

SLOW-ASS ATM USER

For the most part, we are big fans of automatic teller machines. Sure, they charge $300 a pop, but sometimes you need cash at 4:36 a.m. Last time we checked, one-legged Wookiee bookies don't take Discover Card. Unfortunately, our love affair with robot bank servants evaporates when we encounter the backside of Slow-Ass ATM User.

How SAAU magically appears exactly eight nanoseconds before we need to withdraw is beyond us. But one thing's for sure: If you find yourself behind this escargot, you might as well set up base camp. By the time buddy balances his entire IRA, checks the balance of his 64 accounts, transfers money to Budapest, and beats Tetris, aliens will have turned Earth into their own private Six Flags and you'll never see your family again, let alone make it back to Sugar with the 40 bucks you owe.

One of these fart turtles is just waiting to slow you down, and when this happens, you should be ready. Forget trying to withdraw the Benjamins and focus on depositing a couple Andrew Jacksons directly to his moneymaker. Just remember to keep the receipt.

DRUG BUZZKILL

From the moment Cro-Magnon picked up the first pipe, dropped the first tab, snorted the first line, and licked the first frog, there has being somebody lurking in the mist. Waiting . . . watching . . . searching for the right moment to pounce and deliver the fatal blow that ruins your buzz like a faulty condom during a weekend in Vegas. Ladies and gentlemen, Cheech and Chong, we present to you, Drug Buzzkill.

Snatching a wonderful hallucination from the grips of your mind by bringing up the Rwandan genocide just minutes before you slide into a K-Hole, DB is a universal thorn in the side of stoned mankind. Bam! Just like that, your flying carpet comes crashing down faster than Mase's priesthood. What was going to be 14 hours of laughing your lungs off to the sound of the radiator has now been replaced with existential freak-outs, all thanks to the schmuck who brought up the effect of cancer on the human brain right after an eight ball.

Dealing with a trip terminator means confronting the culprit head-on. The minute DB brings you down with a quip about still living in your parent's basement, simply pack a bong that brings *him* down to the hospital.

PEOPLE WHO
DON'T
DESERVE IT

For every one million assholes exists a
baby Jesus who deserves a Fruit Roll-Up.

PARTY ENHANCER

Some people are born with gifts—an uncanny
knowledge of math, a super-speed cross-
word puzzle mind, laser eyes—all great.
But in the end, none can hold a
flame to Party Enhancer, the one
attendee who can take even
the dullest social gathering
and turn it into a patented
Sean John wet dream.

How Party Enhancer
achieves such results is unknown. Thousands have tried to
replicate this innate awesomeness and each has failed. So if you happen
to have a PE in your circle of friends, show them the love they deserve.
Otherwise, you run the risk of never having fun again . . . in your life. Then
you'll die.

There's nothing worse than a cold shoulder to the face as you try to leave the train for work. It reminds you:

a. You have to go to work.

b. Work is in a cubicle.

c. Said cubicle is in Islamabad.

And that's a long-ass commute. Made even longer by the sexually frustrated rams who charge their way onto the train before anyone even exits, like trying to stuff a squab into a turducken. There's only so much room, people!

We just don't get it. It's almost as if these humans aren't really human at all, but in fact brainless salmon beings, desperately trying to swim upstream any chance they get. What's the rush, anyway? All that's waiting for you in the tin can are hoodlums selling overpriced used M&M's and the numbers of several immigration/divorce/injury/eyelash overgrowth lawyers (which, actually, is kind of a pressing matter).

When faced with a subway spawning, the best way to clear a path through these creepy fish folk is to cast a couple right hands and see who bites.

Nobody can deny the thrill of a little healthy attention—a hug from the missus, a kiss from the boyfriend, maybe even a three-day Utah swingers convention in your honor. It's a nice little reminder that we're not just the failed novelists/RadioShack salespeople we see in the mirror each morning. But some freaks take the whole "I love you" thing way too far, like, "I love you, and I'm going to eat your skin."

Come out, Stalker! You can't hide behind that hedge forever. We are on to you and your heavy breathing, so look out, Buddy Binoculars. There is nothing funny about the handwritten envelope we received containing a sample of your back hair and a drawing of you with a pig's body. Well, the pig body might have given us a little chuckle. Seriously, Creepsmear, enough is enough. You do know that every panty sniffer doesn't get to reenact the rollercoaster scene in *Fear* with Reese Witherspoon, right?

Here's what we're thinking, psychos: Drop the loony routine and we promise to stop investing in landmine technology for our front yard. Sound good? Great, because the only other option is to stalk you right back, and you do not want a batch of these fingernails showing up in your face mailbox. They're filthy.

NO CLEANUP NAIL CLIPPER

Sadder than the fact that this crumb ball exists is the likelihood that if you've come in contact with No Cleanup Nail Clipper, you're probably living with the scumbag. Brother, sister, mother, father, roommate, ghost in the basement—no matter, because once you step out of the shower and onto a fresh-cut clipping, NCNC goes from friend to foe faster than a CIA-installed president with knowledge of who whacked JFK.

Under the guise of hygiene, these toe talon litterbugs go about their business, leaving nail shrapnel everywhere. Oblivious to the filth they're creating and the sharpness of their extremities, they leave more mines behind than the entire Korean Demilitarized Zone. Think you're safe outside the bathroom? Think again. The most prolific of the NCNCs have been known to leave DNA droppings from the kitchen to the couch. This isn't Hansel and Gretel, NCNC; where is your little path of nail surprises leading you? The bathroom? The garage? The sex swing shack out back? Bet it's somewhere special, what with the Oregon Trail of toe clippings you're forging.

No Cleanup Nail Clipper must be stopped. Next time you find a deposit, quell the blind rage and follow the nail trail all the way to the source. Once there, make sure to clip the clipper right between the eyes. Just clean that shit up when you're done.

PEOPLE
WHO DESERVE IT
THROUGH TIME

Eventually, someone will invent a time machine. So get ready because
the past and the future are equally littered with heinousness.

GUY WHO STARTS WORLD WAR III

Everyone, meet John Jacob Johnson. You don't know him, but your great-great-grandkids certainly will. See, they'll recognize Old JJJ as the two-timing flying car salesman who'll decide he's had enough of President Timberlake's friendliness with the prime minister of West Korea and throw a pipe bomb at Kim Jong Il 97. Before you know it, peeps will be tossing nukes like an after-school snowball fight. Once the dust settles, France, Qatar, and the moon will be missing, and we're pretty sure half of Britain will have floated away. Thanks a lot, Johnny; our future selves will have to do without bland sausage toast.

Thankfully there is a way to stop this; all we need to do is find buddy's great-great-grandfather and alter the course of history with some super special sterilization shots straight to the junk, Terminator style.

Step into our time machine and join us on a journey to 1975 Socialist Cuba. Now take away the anorexic palm trees and the succulent *arroz con pollo*. What are you left with? Exactly—a bunch of moochers who feel entitled to your shit without even so much as a reimbursing back wax. Case in point: Over-the-Shoulder Reader, the literary leech and softcover commie who thinks just because your copy of *Shantaram* is open, he is welcome to a taste.

These reading rebels leave no turf untouched. Subways, buses, planes, and the occasional hedonistic spa—all fair game for a wasabi-breathing word thief. What fuels his persistent prose poaching remains widely unknown. Maybe he never grew up with books, or maybe he's addicted to the smell of human hair. Maybe a librarian touched his table of contents. Who knows? One thing is for sure; OTSR seems about as scared of owning his own reading materials as the state of Alabama.

Well, we're done enduring the heavy backseat onion breath. Either these degenerate novel digesters start shoplifting their own shit from Scholastic, or we're going to impose a tariff. And the going rate for sneaking a peek of *Eat, Pray, Love* is approximately Fist, Foot, Indian Burn to the face. And that's before adjusting for inflation.

UNDERCOVER STD GIVER

Everybody regrets humping someone—a roommate, a sibling, an aardvark—yet no one-night stand leaves as bad a taste in your mouth, vulva, or groin, as Undercover STD Giver.

Unlike regular STD Givers, this infested gorilla-dick chooses to fornicate only when his sores and boils are sleeping dormant like Punxsutawney Phil after a night at the Gopher Grind and a pawful of pixie dust. Three months later, you wake up with an itchy axe wound and the faint memory of some dude named Paulie feeding you six beers chased with a car bomb. We wish we weren't speaking from experience, but holy Pabst Blue Ribbon, do we associate Panama City with a monthly sandpaper itch that would make Bob Vila scream.

If Undercover STD Giver pulls the gonorrhea over your eyes, there's really only one thing you can do: track him down, tie him up, and let the hookers loose. Y'all know what happened to the Sham-Wow guy.

magine this—you're late for a casting to be the next nose of Nasonex, when suddenly and without warning the Canadian dental internist in front of you brings his sweater vest to a halt, shattering your nasal cavity on impact with his solidified rattail. Your career is ruined. Your family will starve. And it's all thanks to Abrupt Stop Walker.

What's the problem, ASW? Feel an itch in your tongue ring coming on? Spot your girlfriend scarfing 12 cheesy Gordita Supremes in the alley behind Taco Bell? Because those would be the only two acceptable excuses for your abrupt stopping. If everyone stopped mid-stride whenever they damn well felt like it, there would be ten-person pileups all over the world, and Rudy Giuliani can only clean up one place at a time.

If we ever catch you walking like a yellow cab again, we're gonna teach your ass what abrupt means by stopping our five knuckles with your good eye. Maybe then you'd reconsider standing in the middle of a crowded staircase to answer a call from your psychic. (Also, if she didn't see the punishment coming, you might want to look into finding someone new.)

For as long as peeps have being playing with balls, one porker has always taken it upon himself to bogart the sphere for the entire game. A court klepto, if you will, who feels he (or she) is the only person on the planet capable of winning the coed beer league after-work pickup game. While there have been many such individuals through history—Dom DeLuise, Muggsy Bogues, and Nancy Regan, to name a few—we of course refer to them collectively as Ball Hogs.

While it is relatively easy to spot a Ball Hog, with his hands sewn to the side of the Spalding like an old man to a tough-actin' Tinactin canister, it is hard to determine why he exists. Why, BH, do you feel the need to pull an Elian Gonzales every time you get your hands on the ball? Did someone rip Monarchy Barbie from your hands right as you prepared for the most epic tea party of the season? We'd like to know, because we didn't spend $500 just to get a rec-sports T-shirt 42 sizes too big. Pass us the rock!

Pay attention, Piggy; we are only going to draw up this one play. You continue holding on to the biscuit like a fat kid after Lent, and we are going to run a backside, double reverse, loopy loop to the face. Ready . . . break!

8:36 a.m. So far, you've lost 26 minutes on the platform, missed four trains, and contracted some kind of infection from the smell of cured urine. But it's cool, because the dude whose armpit will be in your face for the next half hour is blasting Staind from his portable space-age music device.

As much as we love epic, early 1990s rip-off radio rock, it's just too fucking early. That goes for you, too, No Limit Soldiers. And all the rest of you lowlifes who insist on pushing your musical tastes on the poor morning commuter, like an early-bird Jehovah's Witness.

Should you get pressed against this tool-bag like a curdled ricotta prosciutto panini, make sure you turn up the volume. On his face. Hard to hear with all that ringing in your ears isn't it, buddy?

SPECIAL ENTRY!

PEOPLE WHO
DON'T
DESERVE IT

For every one million assholes exists a
baby Jesus who deserves a Fruit Roll-Up.

CABLE GUY WHO GIVES YOU FREE CHANNELS

As you read this, there are more than three zillion television channels, and it looks like you have them all. Not because you've mortgaged the duplex in Corpus Christi, but because you had a satellite angel beam into your foyer. His name: Cable Guy Who Gives You Free Channels. His unselfish deed: hooking you up with the Trump package for a mere 20 bucks and your dead goldfish, Paco. With two simple twists of a Phillips head, not only are you basking in the pornish glory of the Estonian Playboy channel but also enjoying extensive coverage of the Bhutan premier elephant polo league. *Ka drin che!*

So, next time you find yourself in the presence of Saint Cable Giver, don't shy from his Cool Water intervention. Embrace. Otherwise you'll be forced to supply the entire family with live renditions of the Hustler Channel Xmas Special, Mexican tap dancing, and *Golden Girls* reruns.

MOST PUNCH-WORTHY TIME OF DAY

MOST 8:34 AM   12:16 AM   3:54 AM   5:29 PM   25:43   LEAST

an lives and dies by his words. From the moment he mumbles *Mommy* to the time he screams *mommy-fudger*, his words define him like a "Spring Break 2006!" tattoo. So when some vernacular Wynonna makes off with your favorite slogan, you have every right to get angry as . . . Wait, what's the expression? Oh yeah . . . as fuck.

And why not? You've worked hard to carve out those classic catchphrases. It couldn't have been easy to work "tomato slut" into every sentence over the past five years. You've earned the right to claim "you go, french fry" and "burlap Mexican Santa Claus" as your own. But does Expression Jacker listen? 'Course not. EJ is too busy stealing your dialect quicker than the Hamburglar steals, well, anything. Next thing you know, your entire act is spewing out another man's cake hole.

What to do with a stingy-finger speech stealer? Well, we have one idea; it involves three spatulas, two Latin dictionaries, and one flight to a non-extradition country. "Thank Jesus for Burkina Faso" is one expression that's on the house.

PERSONAL BUBBLE INVADER

Known across the land by many descriptive monikers—space intruder, face raider, close talker, tongue licker—Personal Bubble Invader is a universally assholic character, crossing all borders and speaking all languages. Even Canadian.

Easily identified by the inability to put even the slimmest amount of space between him and people who aren't him, PBI wastes no time getting all up in your grill. So close is his proximity, you can literally smell his stomach lining. It smells like death. And chimichurris. Just because PBI was raised by Latvian breath checkers doesn't mean we should have to get braces and roll in seal feces just to get a little personal space.

If for some reason you should find yourself being accosted by PBI, politely remind him that your no-fly zone is patrolled by swinging fists to the face.

FACEBOOK QUIZ ADDICT

Remember in high school when you would do all the *Cosmo* quizzes to see what your make-out style was and then you'd tell the other two girls sleeping over and they would giggle and roll their eyes because they knew you totally made up the answers so you'd end up the "Smooth Sailor" when really you were more the "Toothy Tyrant" type?

Well, this is kind of like that, only this social networking tycoon takes all the quizzes on the Internet, subsequently alerting every carbon-based life form on the planet, including their aunt and uncle who just joined Facebook. Nothing welcomes Auntie Ruth to the World Wide Web quite like discovering her favorite nephew just took the "What kind of vampire are you?" quiz and got "The gay kind!"

If FQA is a regular on your news feed, first try passive-aggressive commenting. For example, "I took it, too, and it said I'm the 'Punches You in the Face' Vampire." And if he or she is too dense to properly interpret this warning, follow through with your own Dennis Hopper/*Speed*–style pop quiz, asshole. You know, the kind that ends with Keanu Reeves's tongue down your throat.

PRETENTIOUS INDIE MUSIC KNOW-IT-ALL

It's amazing how far some will go to appear awesome, isn't it? Tribal tattoos, Christian Audigier face replacement surgery, drum circles—they're all valiant efforts, but none compares to Pretentious Indie Music Know-It-All, the aging hipster who looks down on anyone and everyone who enjoys recognizable sounds or any tune not sung by a sexually ambiguous lead singer or fat drummer.

Sorry we haven't heard of Black Tiger Face Palace, Onion Rockets, or Butt Hole Soy—that new Brooklyn band with the suspended Harpouditar (look it up). We've been too busy being employed, hygienic, and sociable.

Listen, a good banger from the underground gets us hot and not-bothered too, but make us feel like a sellout for preferring Peter Gabriel to some band that puts cats in a blender and you've gone too far.

So how about you stop being a 31-year-old virgin and come join us on the dance floor? Otherwise, useless musical knowledge won't be the only thing you'll be spitting out of your piehole. Plus, they're playing Simply Red!

PEOPLE
WHO DESERVE IT
THROUGH TIME

Eventually, someone will invent a time machine. So get ready, because the past and the future are equally littered with heinousness.

Man has always had to earn a living. Shit, the pterodactyl wings didn't just magically appear on the cave table. But hunting and gathering are not the grinds with which we take issue. Our beef is with the impotent fancy-pants who decided our destiny would be best spent slaving away inside fluorescently lit buildings with too-close urinals and a handful of people we regularly fantasize about having sex with, but who actually repulse us in real life.

Genius thinking, Guy Who Invented Work. We, too, would rather be inputting the quarterly numbers into this here spreadsheet than cruising for tail, blasting Foreigner, and sucking back beedies. What the T-4 were you thinking, GWIW? Did the advent of the paperclip excite you to the point of organizing all of life around it? Because we're pretty sure there are better ways to waste 40 hours a week. Like the online Kanawake casino.

Next time we take a YouPorn break, you'd better watch your back, because we're climbing into the DeLorean and taking a trip to whenever you're from and not hitting the brakes until you're clocked out.

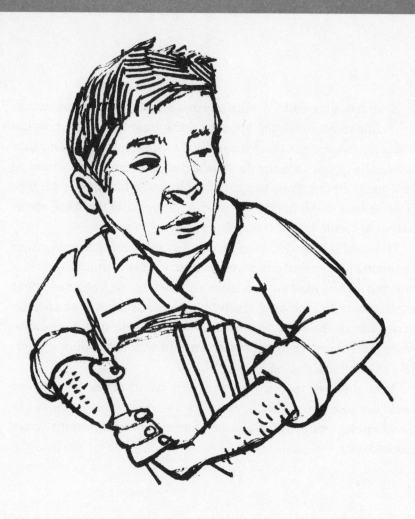

As is the case for Von Dutch models, lower forms of society frequently accost us on the streets begging to borrow our rhinestone earmuffs and skull-embroidered turtlenecks. And who can blame them? We look amazing. But generosity has an expiration date, and we only get a 20 percent discount at the outlet. So when Full-Time Borrower makes off with our hand-braided, snake-embroidered Ethiopian silk panties, shit hits the fan.

Who do you think you are, FTB? We paid for those duds with our own trust-fund money. Then you come along with your "Please, I'm so poor and fragile and I just got ripped off by a Hot Nut vendor with a Garfield fetish," and expect us to forget we lent you our cone-bra out of the goodness of our hearts? Pshaw! The best things in life may be free, but our gold-lined fishnet onesie comes with a Chinese-size trade tariff.

The universe is small, you thieving fiend, and sooner or later we will run into you wearing our V-neck at an underground poetry slam. And you will pay. You will pay like those before you, with a wet towel to the temple. Good luck mooching another garter belt with the international scumbag sign bejeweled on the side of your face.

TRAIL MIX PILLAGER

Before the pygmies of the Ikupuriki rain forest invented trail mix, they spent six years locked in a tree house working on the perfect recipe. When eaten together, the ingredients would provide the ultimate fuel for tiny-people hikes and miniature break dancing. But before they knew it, all the sultanas and almonds were gone, leaving nothing but a pile of sunflower seed paste and the essence of goji berry skins.

The culprit? None other than lowly Trail Mix Pillager, the selfish snacker whose sole purpose in life is to siphon the M&M's out of the gorp, throwing the whole mixture off, like when Jay-Z poached Beyoncé, leaving Kelly Rowland and the other one to host QVC's Vacuum Hour and hawk Mongolian State College lanyards, respectively.

If TMP had stayed in school, he would understand the importance of ratios. But since he dropped out to pillage Nature's Valley, maybe it's time for a beginner lesson. More specifically, plugging his left ear canal with overcooked pasta noodles and letting him feel the imbalance.

BIKER WHO THINKS HE'S A CAR

et's face it: Every so often, people like to pretend they're some-one else. Whether it's an erotic Parisian puppeteer or a blond tap dancer named Doris, if it gets you off, we're all for it.

Unless you happen to be a cyclist suffering an identity crisis, weaving down the middle of the road like a cracked-out chicken who forgot the end of the joke. What the wicker basket, biker? You're not *das auto*. So curb the pompous Duke of York routine and move your powdered wig to the side. Equally entitled or not, you max out at 20 miles per hour and have the width of a malnourished child. How about you use a little common sense and move to the side of the lane so us obese Tonka Trucks don't have to worry about annihilating your selfish flanneled ass?

Sure, biking is great for the environment and shit, but if you don't start sharing the road soon, your sprocket is going to get smashed something fierce. And not in the progressive German way.

SPECIAL ENTRY!

PEOPLE WHO
DON'T
DESERVE IT

For every one million assholes exists a
baby Jesus who deserves a Fruit Roll-Up.

ANYONE OVER 100

In some countries, turning 100 gets you a letter from the Queen, free bingo Tuesdays, and a lifetime supply of Cialis for the next six days you live. Yet here in North America, we leave the geriatrics to tough it out in weird-smelling homes manned by abusive nurses who put Ben Stiller's *Happy Gilmore* role to shame. This is no way to treat a person who has lived through 14 world wars, asbestos, and the beaver-skin condom's rise to prevalence as an acceptable form of contraception.

Plus, shouldn't these old bats be getting some credit for not offing themselves after 365,000 days of *M*A*S*H* reruns and short walks in parks? Science may be curing diseases, but it's sure making it hard for peeps to die. So do a crazy old bitch a solid every now and then. Offer to help her cross the street and slip her some tongue while you're at it. A little light petting goes a long way.

SPECIAL ENTRY!

PEOPLE WHO
DON'T
DESERVE IT

For every one million assholes exists a
baby Jesus who deserves a Fruit Roll-Up.

REAL-LIFE GIANTS

Lately, there's been a lot of midget talk. Little person this and dwarfy dwarf that. Enough already. We get it—the world is big and these people are small in a cute but slightly scary way. But guess what? Little peeps can't help you locate a Lack shelf at an abnormally high-ceilinged IKEA. Nor can they shoo the clouds away with their arms when it's overcast on vacation.

You know who can? Real-Life Giants, that's who. On top of being awesome, RLGs can endure some pretty traumatic life experiences, like puberty at age two and a half and random breast leakage. Yet they get no credit for it. Gheorghe Muresan had a mustache as an embryo and he never brags. Ever. So next time you come face to kneecap with a big friendly giant, show some love by humping that shin like Scooby-Doo does a fire hydrant in heat.

HAVEN'T SEEN YOU IN TEN YEARS FAVOR ASKER

In today's digital age, with the advent of social networking and electronic PO boxes, getting tracked down by an old flame is easier than spotting a Mexican in Poland. And by old flame, we mean the ginger kid from seventh grade whose sweat smelled like DiGiorno. Now he's old. And unemployed. And just happens to be in your line of work. So don't be surprised when you "bump" into him in the chat room on OiledAccountingStuds.com. "How serendipitous," he'll say, while surveying your living room on his self-installed spycam. "Maybe you could get me an interview at Glieber, Goobman, Glickster, and Stein."

Sure, no problem, old not-friend we haven't spoken to since we had the Collective Soul album memorized backward. We'll get right on that. Just after we solve world hunger, snowshoe across Africa, and learn how to make a wicked Bellini. Shouldn't take too long. Get back to us on November 6, 2187 and we'll be sure to stuff your resume in the boss's hologram sandwich (which is how sandwiches will be eaten in 2187).

TERRIBLE BABY NAMER

Birthing a human is no small feat. In 2005, a Brazilian woman pushed 17 pounds of baby flesh out of her *buceta*. If anyone could rationalize giving her kid a life-ruining name, it's her. But guess what? She named it Bob. Or something. So there really is no excuse for getting knocked up with the intention of releasing Aluminum Foil Jr. into the world nine months later. Chances are poor Foily won't make it out of second grade.

Terrible Baby Namer, this page is for you. Just because Mr. and Mrs. Wiener were high on empty Pam cans when they decided to name you Seymour, doesn't give you the right to take out your pent-up childhood traumas on your own offspring. That's called transference, and our headshrinker says it's pretty effed up. You'd better believe that when Wanna Towell is reaching for the soap in the slammer after burning down a private school wearing nothing but a peacoat, it won't be anybody's fault but your own.

A piece of advice, TBN: Next time you're forced into a threesome with Gwyneth Paltrow and Sylvester Stallone, better call shotgun on "John Smith" quick. Otherwise, veto power is going to dub your lovechild Apple Moonblood and we're going to have to change your name manually. To Smushed Face.

PEOPLE
WHO DESERVE IT
THROUGH TIME
Eventually, someone will invent a time machine. So get ready, because
the past and the future are equally littered with heinousness.

Kids today take everything for granted—long-lasting gum, human rights, bar nuts. But perhaps the most abused luxury is the cellular telephone, a powerful device made popular by Michael Douglas, used to contact others in case of an emergency. Like, "Oh no, is that my BFF's house being set aflame? Better call to warn her on my cellular telephone."

In the days of yore, such technological wonders did not exist, and to warn your favorite uncle of an impending terrorist attack on uncles, you had to put a quarter in a box-shaped machine hidden, unmarked, on the streets. And when you finally found the magical ringer, there was Pay Phone Hog, clogging the wires with tales of last night's rave at the local slaughterhouse. Meanwhile, your uncle had been kidnapped and his moustache waxed in the shape of Texas.

If you're experiencing an emergency anywhere between 1899 and 1999 and stuck behind PPH, free up some airtime with a long-distance call to the cornea. And don't forget your antibacterial wipes. Those oldies are loaded with mites.

ealth is one of those things you can't live without—like two-bite brownies, or the 2001 *Best of Sade* album. Without it, we're nothing but non-alcoholic, less fun versions of Harry Dean Stanton. So when we get sick, we take it seriously. But not as seriously as Extreme Hypochondriac, the boy who cried wolf, only "wolf" is cancer and "cried" is cried.

Convinced every bodily malfunction is a harbinger of death, Extreme Hypochondriac is always on the verge of croaking. A paper cut is a flesh-eating disease. A mosquito bite, a brain tumor. A small bump on the hooch, warts. The more this overexaggerator spirals into lunacy, the more we wish he would just contract the fake Ebola virus from that Morgan Freeman movie already and have his energy reserves too depleted to talk about it.

If we have to hear a hangnail described as lupus one more time, we're going to take the scalpel into our own hands and conduct this checkup freestyle. And believe us, it's going to involve highly invasive and unnecessary procedures, performed with instruments rusty enough to give an iron-oxidized nail tetanus. Maybe then Extreme Hypochondriac will think next time he cries Parkinson's.

Okay, before everyone freaks out and threatens to drag us to the guillotine, let's take a moment to think about this one like the mature, only-reading-this-book-because-their-significant-other-is-on-the-can folk we are. Cool? Cool.

Being badgered to death by some self-righteous poli-sci student on your way to work (massage parlor) is not the best way to kick off the day. Especially when you know they only signed up to get the free T-shirt and the chance to perv on some hippie tail from a different angle.

When it comes to the environment, we're more Al Gore than Exxon *Valdez*. It just happens that this guy chooses the most irritating two seconds of our lives to assault us with his clipboard of doom. We're sorry we don't have a second to save the indigenous box possum of Madagascar, but we're late for a custody case, so back the hemp bracelet off, Granola Jar.

Instead of saddling us with the guilt of walking out on Mother Nature, how about you and your patchouli oil go back to the commune. We'll donate on our own time, but only after we make a tax-deductible donation to your face.

EXPRESS CHECKOUT CHEATER

People try to get away with a lot of shit these days: not paying taxes, excessive drug use, selling the Illinois junior Senate seat. And most of the time we're okay with it. What doesn't check the kosher box is the d-bag who thinks she can bring 36 items through the express line, ignoring the giant "12 Items or Less" sign, like subway turnstile jumpers ignore the law.

Well, guess what? We're onto you Express Checkout Cheater. We see the extra 16 ramen packs you have hidden under the milk, even if the cashier doesn't. And if you think we are going to sit idly by while you abuse the leniency of Whole Foods, you have another think coming. Shit's about to get real organic up in this business.

Here's the 411, ECC: Next time you're 79 items over the limit, you'd better watch your back, because someone is watching you, and you're about to get 12 or more punches delivered straight to your fruit basket.

We let kids get away with a lot of shit—screaming like homicide victims for no apparent reason, touching pigeons, actually running away with a handful of shit—but as they age, these actions become less acceptable and more associated with Courtney Love. However, one behavior seems to stick, like a gaggle of tweens to a Miley Cyrus hot dog. And that shit-disturbing characteristic takes on a human form in Tattletale, the self-righteous narc who fills the day incriminating innocent fun-havers.

Like an Enron employee with no friends and a hairless cat, this whistle-blower will divulge your darkest secrets for a little attention and the chance to talk to another human without the aid of a webcam. Does Tattletale benefit in any way from telling your boyfriend that sometimes you make out with the Blair Underwood poster in the window of the Blockbuster near your apartment? Only if she's going steady with that particular window, and that seems unlikely given glass's track record with interracial dating.

Chances are Tattletale has already outed you on more than one occasion. How do you think the boss found out about your bikini-wax side business in stall three? Or that sometimes you sleep under your desk after huffing printer cartridges? So next time you catch a snitch opening his filthy piehole, make that shit a la mode with a scoop of fist to the face.

GROWN MAN WHO REFUSES TO EAT CRUSTS

Here's the thing: Crusts are just the ends of bread. So what the hell is wrong with you, Grown Man Who Refuses to Eat Crusts? We understand children like their crusts removed, but that's only because kids are stupid. Do you also eat pennies off the floor, and put your fingers in electric sockets? (If yes, please forgive us; we didn't realize you were retarded.)

But if not, we have some advice. Keep chopping the edges off your Wonder bread, and you're never going to get laid again. In fact, you're going to have so little sex that you'll probably punch yourself in the face. Maybe you could use your discarded crusts to construct a makeshift eye patch. AARGH!*

---

* A makeshift eye patch can be constructed by balling up the discarded crusts, adding two teaspoons of water, and pressing in an overpriced European panini maker. Let cool. Apply to eye.

Nothing screams mama's boy like a man who prides himself on knowing where to get the perfect liquid nitrogen salmon mousse. Except maybe a man who imports his truffle oil from Sri Lankan mushroom poachers and then bathes in it for three days to make a human marinade so strong, he ends up pairing himself with a robust red and gnawing off his own limbs.

Yes, that's right. It's time to meet Pretentious Foodie, a modern breed of tool-face so disenchanted with the pitiful taste of the bourgeois palate, he consumes only the most ridiculous forms of sustenance and then word vomits it on anyone who will listen. Too busy trying to make the most of his $95 diamond-infused cherry tomato entrée with dressing on the side, this turducken doesn't have time for the common culinary pleasures of the everyman. Plus, he has to be on a plane to Tuscany tomorrow to experience *sous-vide* guido glands firsthand.

Who the Boston Market side dish do you think you are, PF? Unless the answer is that guy who hosts every show on the Food Network, we're guessing you're nobody. So step off your pork pedestal or risk having your aged cheddar puree stuffed up your fairy-glazed muttonchops. Bon appétit.

INCESSANT FACEBOOK STATUS UPDATER

So-and-so is baking chocolate chip banana cupcakes. So-and-so is feeding her Siamese cats. So-and-so has nothing better to do than to sit in front of her computer and report meaningless crap that clogs our news feed. So-and-so is Incessant Facebook Status Updater, and she is going to disrupt your life like a bad case of the black lung before your Medieval Times audition.

So intent on sharing every gory detail of her tiny little life, this verbal vomiter does not leave her computer for more than four minutes at a time. When the tickets get booked it's all, "Kokomo, here I come!" When the gym membership gets renewed it's an uploaded "before" picture. And when she finally takes a shit after eating that giant turkey leg, you can bet details of its quality and consistency will be provided for the masses. How can we continue to stalk our exes if every time we go online we're slapped in the face by another update on the health of Christine, the lactose-intolerant hamster? It's this type of interwebular behavior that makes us want to go back in time, grab a typewriter, and bust the keys out on Al Gore's www-inventing face.

While it may seem impossible to stop Incessant Facebook Status Updater at this moment, we promise there is a team of underage Indian hackers working around the clock. Until then you'll have to settle for the satisfaction that comes with knowing her 222 other "friends" also want to punch IFSU in the Facebook.

nglish has always been the world's lingua franca. For all you PhD dropouts, that means the language two people who don't share a mother tongue use to communicate with each other. And judging by this new "Theory of Globalization," peeps gonna be talkin' lots of de English. But just because the language is of West Germanic descent, it doesn't give some speakers the right to enforce its rules like a cafeteria monitor at a prison.

Stand down, Grammar Nazi. It's hard enough for us to sound coherent after that five-hour absinthe-tasting tour, let alone re-member every obscure Old Norse rule the Vikings invented when they were bored on their ice floe to Constantinople. No, we don't know when to say "whom," or why *I* comes before *E*, except after *P. D?* And you know why? Because we're too busy not being assholes, that's why.

Our subjects don't agree with your verbs, if you know what we mean. So get off your oral high horse and shove your pronouns up your semicolon. And if that solution doesn't work for you, here's a different preposition: Keep correcting our run-on sentences and we'll rearrange your sentence structure so the only adjective left to describe your face is "eek!"

DIGITAL CAMERA VIEWING STEALER

When last's night party has come and gone, and all that remains are the faint smears of Day-Glo body paint and the essence of goulash, it's nice to have a memory-capturing box to help you put the pieces together. Like waking up Christmas morning, ripping off the wrapping paper, and discovering you had a threesome with the landlord and his cat, a morning-after digi-log can change your life. That is, until Digital Camera Viewing Stealer shows up and demands to see the naked *Facts of Life* trivia picture, only to bogart the camera for the rest of eternity.

"I'll give it back," the crook will say before hijacking your screen, losing your place, and clicking so far back through your life, she ends up in your mother's uterus with 13 megapixels and a 3x zoom lens sharp enough to deep-fry the placenta. Dang, DCVS! Why you gotta be like that? We were so close to figuring out how we got this bag of unmarked bills and that IHOP-shaped hickey.

If you ever snatch our cyber souvenirs out from under our noses again, we're going to give you a dose of nostalgia you'll never forget. Which is a nice way of saying you'll have a permanent clicking in your jaw and a photo album titled "Blood Face." Say "cheese curds!"

PERPETUAL ASS KISSER

If you have ever been to high school or held down a j-o-b, there is a 99.9 percent chance you've come across this slimer. In fact, the only way you could have avoided him is if you happen to live under the sea with a family of Swiss robots. And even then, we're pretty sure there would still be some robot nose penetrating some robot ass. Yup, like Puff Daddy in the 1990s or fear in the 2000s, Perpetual Ass Kisser is everywhere, because as long as there's an ass to kiss, there will be someone getting on his or her knees.

Don't get us wrong—we understand to get ahead you've got to pucker up to a keester every once in a while. (How do you think we got this book deal? Thanks, Uncle Jim ☺.) But that doesn't mean we go around sucking up to every teacher, boss, or vending machine salesman in the tristate area. Like a smart missile, bum-massaging is a targeted operation. PAK? More like the nuclear bomb of brown-nosing. When confronted they'll never admit it, choosing instead to respond with, "What are you talking about? That's not shit on my mouth; it's chocolate."

While there are many ways to deal with Perpetual Ass Kisser, we tend to lean toward the traditional. Remember, there are no short-cuts in life. So if this prostate masseur thinks he's going to sneak his way through the back door, we're going to make sure the only thing he'll be kissing is his modeling career as it waves buh-bye.

COMPUTER CUSTOMER SERVICE

At some point we've all lost a credit card, had to change a flight, or placed an order for a life-size latex love robot. So we pick up the phone, dial the 1-800 number, finalize our skin-color preference, and wait to speak with a helpful Kurdish call center operator. Unfortunately, instead of explaining to Uri that our Chase Sapphire card must have flushed itself down the toilet at Tim Hortons, we're left jumping through hoops because he's been snuffed out by the evil Computer Customer Service.

Long ago, inventing a compu-bot that could handle all of man's menial tasks probably seemed like a nifty idea. Why pay some humanoid $6 an hour to answer the phone and fart, when you could pay a circuit board zip? Seemed like the right solution. Wrong! Now we're all forced to endure the humiliation of being bossed around by a talking toaster, just so we can stay one more night at the Days Inn, Atlantic City. And if being treated like a toddler isn't bad enough, CCS makes us repeat ourselves six billion times, ensuring everyone in the office knows our secret password is "Mr. Huggles."

Thanks a bunch, tyrannical Hal. Next time we pick up and you're on the other end, we're going to punch the keypad so hard, not even pressing zero will save you.

A fortune cookie once told us, "If you love something, let it leave; if it comes back, it's meant to be!" What it failed to mention is sometimes you don't get to let your love leave. Sometimes your love leaves you, and sometimes it's on the arm of a dragon tattoo model with rock-hard abs and a pink tricycle.

Ladies and gentlemen, people of Lavalife, allow us to introduce Lover Thief, the two-bit coworker/roommate/dentist who swoops in and snatches your significant other from under your non-toned biceps. Sure, you'll tell yourself you can do better, that there are more fish in the sea, and that your ex lover probably had crabs, but it doesn't change the fact that LT has been premeditating sex with your boo for the last six months. And yes, there are plenty of singles in Greater Milwaukee, but booty burglar only has a taste for forbidden fruit, and shnookums just happened to be in season.

While at times it may seem impossible to stop Lover Thief from ripping out your heart, fear not, dear sulker. Simply pull your head out of the Häagen-Dazs tub and strike Casanova Klepto with a double scoop of chocolate chip to the cookie dough.

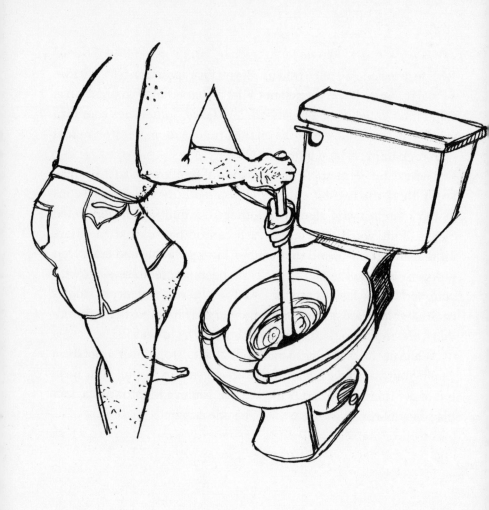

PHANTOM TOILET CLOGGER

One nice thing about being human is that regardless of your opinion on the relative babeness of Jessie Spano vs. Lisa Turtle, at the end of the day we all have the same living nightmare: throwing down a double deuce after lunch at the burrito barn and having the porcelain gods betray you.

What separates the shitters from the shitheads is how a pooper deals with the aforementioned snafu. And some of us treat the scene like a badly directed hit-and-run in "I Still Still Know What You Did the Summer Before You Spent the Whole Time Trying to Forget What You Did the Summer Before." Aww, yeah, we're talkin' 'bout Phantom Toilet Clogger, the foul jungle beast who leaves his mark in your toilet without so much as a peep. Yessir, he sneaks off into the night, throwing you into the hot seat the next time a member of your Books About Oprah's Book Club Club saunters into the WC. "It wasn't me," you'll assert. But by that time, PTC will be across the border with a new passport, a mail-order bride, and a discount Andy Kaufman wig from the Rug Hut.

With the advent of DNA testing, fingerprinting technology, and bounty hunters, it is now possible to track down a feces fugitive. But that means taking a sample, and you'd better believe that when we find this assailant, we'll be returning the evidence.

NO SPECIFIC TIME DELIVERY GUY

When Al Gore dreamed up a network of talking computers that could send each other stuff over a bunch of invisible nets, we bet he was most excited for the chance to have a case of Orville Redenbacher's special popcorn delivered directly to his house in under 12 hours without the hassle of making small talk with a worker at the Cleveland Cinematheque. What he didn't envision was the whole concept getting demolished by a dillydallying truck driver in a one-piece suit and a hankering for a sloppy joe.

God damn you, No Specific Time Delivery Guy. Do you think we have nothing better to do than to sit around for the next eight hours while you sample the regional slushie selection at every Wawa on the way? Just because we've been unemployed since Lincoln got elected and can recite the *Bold and the Beautiful* credits in chronological order, it doesn't mean we don't have places to be. The food bank closes at four thirty, mofo.

Next time you decide to reinterpret rush delivery, we're going to show you our take on "please sign here." More specifically, leaving our John Hancock on your face. And if you don't get the message the first time, we're going to suggest you come back the next day, anytime between nine and five.

WHAT IF I DESERVE IT?

Listen, we all act like People Who Deserve It some days. Chances are you've caught yourself or been spotted engaging in more than one of the degenerate behaviors depicted in this punchopedia. And if not, you definitely deserve it for contributing to the death of endangered Malaysian oak trees by purchasing this mediocre book. Got you! So, what now? Well, for one thing, you're probably going to get punched in the face.

And that's okay.

Inhaling a knuckle sandwich can be a formative experience but, like Albanian shin stretching, it's best enjoyed in moderation. So when you've been caught behaving badly and are faced with an impending iron fist, better get to know your options:

Option 1: Run

It may be the oldest escape in the book, but if you've got legs, why not use 'em? Plus, it'll kill two birds with one stone. Bird one being the calories in the tuna melt you just gargled in your roommate's bed, and bird two, avoiding looking like the tuna melt you just gargled in your roommate's bed. P.S.: Sorry if you don't have legs.

Option 2: Hide

Such a well-thought-out getaway requires some serious planning time. Which means you must know you've been a little shit and are sidestepping the victim of your shittyness, like an overdue library book that'll now cost you your liver to return. Cowardly as it may seem, this option works. Just ask Osama. And when you do, find out what ever happened to our copy of *Lolita*.

Option 3: Spit

In an eye, up a nose, down a throat. Whatever it takes to fend off a bashing to your bits. Hocking a loogie is both an excellent form of aerobic exercise and a widely accepted form of Singaporean self-defense. So when a swinging wrist enters your line of vision, harness the remnants of your afternoon string cheese and fling it the foot/fist way.

Option 4: Swallow

Nothing says "My balls are the size of Pamela Anderson's sandbags" like looking an assailant straight in the crazy eye, pleading guilty to your crime, and swallowing a brass knuckle straight to the Adam's apple without so much as a Richard-Simmons-after-45-minutes-on-the-elliptical whimper. You go, girl.

DIY PUNCHING BAG

॥॥॥

Not all of us have the backroom brawl experience that comes with growing up on an Indian reservation in Thunder Bay, Ontario. Some of us need practice before we get cracking. That's why we've included this Do-It-Yourself Punching Bag. Simply follow these five easy steps:

Step 1: Draw Enemy

Step 2: Cut Along Dotted Line

Step 3: Name Enemy

Step 4: Tape to Piece of Meat

Step 5: Go to Town

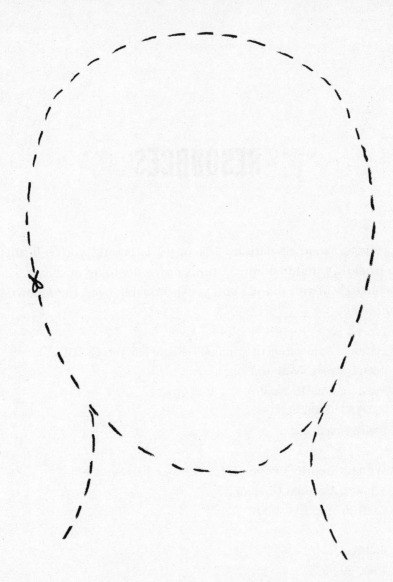

RESOURCES

||||||||||||||||||||||||||||||||||||||||||||||||||||||

Kudos, Good Samaritan: 188 pages later and you've flushed nearly a hundred human turds down the toilet of shame. Unfortunately, if you did it right, you'll probably need the following numbers:

National Association of Criminal Defense Lawyers (NACDL)
1660 L Street NW, 12th Floor
Washington, DC 20036
(202) 872-8600
assist@nacdl.org

Witness Security Division of the U.S. Marshals Service
S. Jones, Assistant Director
(202) 307-9150

Bail Yes
1-800-224-5937

Red Cross
1-800-REDCROSS (1-800-733-2767)

Anger: Wisdom for Cooling the Flames, by Thich Nhat Hanh
Riverhead Trade, 2002

Johnnie Cochran, ESQ
The Cochran Firm
1-800-THE-FIRM

Reconstructive Hand Surgeons of Indiana
(317) 249-2616
www.indianahandsurgeons.com

9-1-1
911

GLOSSARY OF TERMS

Alabama: The 22nd state to join the union, 23rd in population, 30th in land mass, and 58th in mathematics.

Beirut: The capital city of Lebanon and a wonderful place to visit, especially in May on Middle East Airlines—only $699 round trip plus complimentary tabouleh salad! Call Jamila now!

Bollywood: An informal term used to describe the Hindi film industry based in Mumbai, India. Bollywood produces more ~~successful~~ films per year than Steven Spielberg, Harvey Weinstein, and Jenna Jameson combined.

Bromance: A term coined by reality star Brody Jenner to describe the complicated heterosexual bond between two males who are both in love with Brody Jenner.

Buccaneers: Established in 1976, the Tampa Bay Buccaneers lost their first 26 games. It wasn't until midway through the second season that these orange pirates notched up a W.

Buceta: A derogatory Portuguese term for a woman's lady parts that if uttered in public could cost you your *lingua*. Which is also Portuguese, for a different part.

Cheesy Gordita Supreme: A limited availability Taco Bell offering consisting of one beef taco wrapped inside a melted cheese gordita wrapped inside a cheesy baby polar bear skin wrapped inside the biceps of an ultimate fighting champion, stuffed and topped with cheese.

Cymbalta: A prescription drug used to treat depression; Cymbalta is a serotonin-norepinephrine reuptake inhibitor that makes your brain cave feel like apple pie. Unicorns!

David Barton Gym: A chain of physical training facilities, decorated to look like a rave thrown inside a prostate for maximum iron-pumping stimulation. Free sex and hair gel in all locker rooms (Bahrain club excluded).

DiGiorno: A frozen pizza brand created by the Kraft Foods Inc., whose slogan is: "It's not delivery. It's DiGiorno." Contrary to popular belief, its spokesman is not a tanned cyborg with a voicebox; it's Dick Vitale.

DNA (deoxyribonucleic acid): A nucleic acid and the genetic instructions used in the formation of all living organisms. In short, it's the goo that ensures you get the same fat earlobes as your father.

eHarmony: A website that connects lonely people on the Internet based on a 1,289,837-point compatibility system made to wear daters down until they're too tired not to sleep with each other in real life.

Enron: A beacon of American capitalism. In 2001, Enron was caught cooking their books worse than a fondue party with Bobby Flay and Gordon Gecko.

Eyelash moisturizer: A revolutionary eye care product that prevents parched eyelashes from breaking off and blinding you. Nobody likes an eyeless woman.

Gheorghe Muresan: A former professional basketball player and famous Romanian, Muresan's height (7 feet, 7 inches) made him the one of the tallest players in the NBA and led to a starring role in *My Giant*, where he played the giant.

Gold Bond: An over-the-counter skin irritation treatment available as both a powder and a topical cream. Gold Bond is a staple of Jock Itch Anonymous.

Havana: The capital of Cuba used to be Disneyland for gangsters and prostitute aficionados. Now it's more like Knott's Berry Farm for beards and army hat aficionados. Like Williamsburg, Brooklyn. Or Virginia, if you think about it.

IHOP: The International House of Pancakes is a chain of American restaurants founded in 1958 by a five-year-old boy who would only eat things in stacks separated by pats of butter. He now lives in Land O'Lakes.

IKEA: The world's largest furniture supplier, pioneer of self-assembly, and official furniture supplier of Sweden, student dorms, city apartments, country apartments, and basically every dwelling in the world.

Indian Burn: A playground staple involving twisting someone's arm skin in opposite directions and then running away like a girl.

Kathleen Turner: An American actress born in 1954 who rose to fame in the 1980s. She is also the muse of our favorite Austrian techno-pop singer, Falco.

Lick the Frog: A primitive method of getting blitzed, whereby a bored Medieval tween would suck on a toad for its poisonous properties and spend the rest of the evening downing bison-flavored Big Gulps.

Light Petting: Touching, fondling, or caressing above the waist in a sexual way, and sometimes below the waist if you're feeling frisky, but always over the pants. Also, the proper method to show affection to a fragile pet.

Mandolin: A musical instrument in the lute family, made widely popular by Jamie Lee Curtis after she purchased one for husband Christopher Guest, who appreciated the gesture, but never used it much.

Menthols: Magical cigarettes enjoyed by floozies and flavored with a compound called menthol, which acts as a cooling agent, even though it doesn't make anything cool in real life.

Microsoft Excel: One of the original computer programs in the Microsoft Office Suite, designed by Bill Gates to calculate how much money he won't be leaving to his children and also to make tables without legs.

Mohel: A rabbi who specializes in circumcisions at Jewish penis-cutting parties, the third most requested entertainer behind strippers and farting clowns.

Mother Teresa: Born Agnesë Gonxhe Bojaxhiu, this Albanian Catholic nun is basically the goodest person to have ever walked the earth. Sorry, JC.

Olestra: A food chemical invented by Sir Von Snacks-a-Lot, mainly used in baked potato chips, which, when ingested, will cause said baked potato chips to leak from the anus in a clear yet deeply disturbing mucus.

Seitan: A soy product made to resemble meat in texture and taste, enjoyed by Machiavellian vegans who are plotting an evil empire in which everything would look like something else and nothing would be as it seems.

***Shantaram*:** A novel about an escaped convict and heroin addict written by an escaped convict and heroin addict. Like watching a TV on your TV. Trippy, man.

Staind: A mid-1990s Massachusetts rock band followed religiously by cutters, recreational bowling aficionados, and Christine Lehman who has 152 Facebook friends and also really likes Scott Speedman.

Thunderbird: Ford Motors' attempt at evoking the spirit of the Native American mythological creature by having old, white Beach Boys and middle-class American Italians drive around in hand-painted flame mobiles.

Tomato Slut: A woman who sleeps with tomatoes on the first date.

Tough-Actin' Tinactin: An athlete's foot spray that provides the fungus-related answers you've always been looking for, and some you haven't.

Turducken: Heaven comes in the form of a chicken, stuffed into a duck, stuffed into a turkey, served on Thanksgiving to your racist aunt.

Usher: American-born singer/songwriter known mostly for an uncanny ability to control his temperature when shirtless and for surviving a German cat food commercial costarring Naomi Campbell.

Uvulopalatopharyngoplasty: A surgical procedure used to remove parts of the throat including the hangy-ball thingy, which is scientifically known as the uvula. Dirty.

Vajazzle: The equivalent of Bedazzling for your poonany. For external use only (just ask Jennifer Love Hewitt).

Vastus Medialis: One of four quadriceps muscles, used mostly for squatting, lunging, and looking like a prepubescent girl when standing next to Apolo Ohno.

The View: A daytime television program hosted by menopausal women who pretend to like each other, but really spend the whole time screaming about "hot topics" in elastic waistband pants, which they like.

Von Dutch: An American multinational clothing company famous for its ability to put a snake, a skull, an eagle, and rhinestones all on one man's halter top.

Yahoo!: An Internet search engine of early 2000s fame. Today, Yahoo! is mostly home to dangerously wrong advice about bacne and how to get a green card in Mexico.

Yarmulke: A spherical skullcap traditionally worn by observant Jewish men, but later adopted by the occasional puppet and hep cats in Williamsburg, Virginia.

ACKNOWLEDGMENTS

Thank you Hope Deli, little Thai lady at Siam Orchid, the Bluetooth Company, random subway goers and douche-boats, Google Docs, psychotic Internet commenters, suggest-a-punchers, M Shanghai's Kung Pao chicken, stepparents, stepsiblings, real siblings, biological parents, biological parents' flavor of the month, actual friends, friends of friends, estranged relatives, Nicky K, BB, Ramien, Zosef & D-Bomb, Lexy, the 440Js, Panda, Jesse of the Brooklyn Barbell Club, our agent, our editor, our outsourced Indian therapist (Haleema), anyone who's ever looked at us the wrong way, the lady who stepped in wet cement and kept walking on Metropolitan, white-haired stoop guy, the Auschwitz alarm clock, the Canadian government, the First Amendment, Photoshop, Compfight, Montreal bagels, Brita water filters, Skittles, Lactaid, Wordpress, the Dollard move, our real jobs. Oh, and Drano.

NOTES

|||||||||||||||||||||||||||||

Chances are, you come across People Who Deserve It every day. Use this section to keep track of all the tools you meet. Then write a low-budget book!

_____

_____

_____

_____

_____

_____

_____

_____

_____

_____

_____

ABOUT THE AUTHORS

Tim Gordon

Tim Gordon is the author of the soon-to-be international bestseller *People Who Deserve It* (it's the book you're reading now). This is really his only written accomplishment, other than some award-winning advertisements, but who cares, right? Ads rot your brain!

Anyway, Tim is a tall, Canadian-born gentleman who spent most of his childhood living a life of white-bread debauchery in Vancouver, British Columbia, where his mother and father were chocolate architects.

After a brief stint as a construction worker, Tim decided to pursue his passion for material possessions, moving to New York and taking a job at a prestigious advertising agency. His work has been seen on trade websites, some intertubular forum called "YouTube," and the inside of urine-soaked New York City subway cars.

Currently, Tim resides in Brooklyn, New York, where he lives with his writing partner and potential biological sister, and their landlord's two dogs.

Casey Rand

Casey Rand is the author of the soon-to-be international bestseller *People Who Deserve It* (it's the book you're reading now). This is really her only written accomplishment, other than some not-so-award-winning advertisements, but who cares, right? Ads rot your brain!

Anyway, Casey is a tall, Canadian-born gentlewoman who spent most of her childhood living a life of Jewy debauchery in Montreal, Quebec, where her mother and father were real estate disc jockeys.

After a brief stint as a sushi chef, Casey decided to pursue her passion for material possessions, moving to New York and taking a job at a prestigious advertising agency. Her work has been seen on trade websites, some intertubular forum called "YouTube," and urine-soaked New York City billboards.

Currently, Casey resides in Brooklyn, New York, where she lives with her writing partner and potential biological brother, and their landlord's two dogs.